Middle English Poetry
IN MODERN VERSE

Middle English Poetry
IN MODERN VERSE

Translated and Edited
by Joseph Glaser

Hackett Publishing Company, Inc.
Indianapolis/Cambridge

For further information, please address:

Hackett Publishing Company, Inc.
P.O. Box 44937
Indianapolis, IN 46244-0937

www.hackettpublishing.com

Cover design by Joseph Glaser and Abigail Coyle
Text design by Chris Downey
Composition by Agnew's, Inc.
Printed at Edwards Brothers, Inc.

Library of Congress Cataloging-in-Publication Data

Middle English poetry in modern verse / translated and edited
    by Joseph Glaser.
        p. cm.
    Includes bibliographical references and index.
    ISBN-13: 978-0-87220-880-3
    ISBN-13: 978-0-87220-879-7 (pbk.)
    1. English poetry—Middle English, 1100–1500—Modernized
versions.   I. Glaser, Joseph.
    PR1203.M47 2007
    821′.108—dc22

                                        2006033819

The paper used in this publication meets the minimum requirements of
American National Standard for Information Sciences—Permanence of
Paper for Printed Library Materials, ANSI Z39.48–1984

For Anna, Mia, Lily, and M.J.

CONTENTS

Introduction

These Modern English versions of poems from about 1200 to 1500 range from brief lyrics to whole romances, and provide a broad sampling of Middle English poetry. Equally important, they make up a rich collection of works as appealing in their various ways as the more familiar poems of Chaucer and the poet of *Gawain and the Green Knight.*

With one exception, every selection here depends on manuscript evidence for its survival.[1] Most could easily have disappeared along with a great number of other works now lost. Medieval manuscripts were expensive and difficult to produce, so they were never as common as printed books later became. Many were lost, destroyed, or recycled—broken down so the leaves could be scraped clean and rewritten. Some are only partly legible. Because each manuscript was written out by hand, the texts may sometimes be unreliable. A few of the shorter selections appear to be only fragments of longer poems that no longer exist.

But the picture is not nearly as bleak as it might have been. By far the greater part of the poems translated here appear to be finished and accurate versions of what their authors intended. Even the shortest ones (for instance, lyric 2, "All night beside the rose . . .") make satisfying, often memorable reading as they stand. And the texts have been examined and reexamined by scholars. These poems are as close as we are likely to come to hearing their Middle English writers speaking to us across the centuries.

The book starts with lyrics, many of which were meant to be sung and possibly danced to.[2] A number of these are accompanied in manuscripts by their musical settings or appear in pocket-size songbooks compiled by or for professional minstrels. The first two parts, "Worldly Lyrics" and "Snatches," include better than one out of every five items that remain of Middle English secular lyrics. This amounts to more than half the surviving

---

1. The exception is the selection from *The Squire of Low Degree,* for which the manuscript versions have vanished. The poem's earliest appearance now is in a printed edition of 1560.

2. Medieval lyrics are still frequently performed, and there are always a few recordings available—for example, *English Songs of the Middle Ages* by the ensemble Sequentia (Musical Heritage 514451M) or the Hillyard Ensemble's *Medieval English Music* (Harmonia Mundi 1008211). Other performances can be sampled on the Internet or borrowed from libraries.

texts complete enough to make presentable poems. The third part, "Religious Lyrics," draws on a wider pool of preserved work in an attempt to illustrate several types of religious verse from an age steeped in devotional observances and expression.

The rest of the book is made up of longer selections and narrative poems, the Middle English equivalent of modern novels. These are a highly varied lot, covering a range of interests and styles. "Selections," the fourth part, includes substantial passages from four works: *Piers Plowman,* William Langland's book-length satire; *Confessio Amantis,* John Gower's courtly retellings of lovers' tales; *The Squire of Low Degree,* an anonymous romance; and Gavin Douglas's Scottish version of the *Aeneid.* The final section, "Narratives," presents five equally diverse complete poems: *The Land of Cockayne,* a cheerful ecclesiastical burlesque; *Sir Orfeo,* a Breton *lai* in English; *Athelston,* a plain-spoken romance written in the popular tail-rhyme form; *Saint Erkenwald,* a saint's legend in alliterative verse; and *The Cock and the Fox,* Robert Henryson's sophisticated beast fable in rhyme royal.

The language of these poems diverges almost as much as their matter and forms. Middle English ranged from tough, unfamiliar dialects to a speech much closer to Modern English that was in use around London toward the end of the period. Here is a short meditation that most present-day readers would have to struggle to understand:

> Loverd, thu clepedest me
> An ich nagt ne ansuarede thee
> Bute wordes scloe and sclepie.
> "Thole yet! Thole a litel!"
> Bute "yet" and "yet" was endlis,
> And "thole a litel" a long wey is.

> My Lord, when you called out to me,
> I answered nothing back to thee
> But these words, slow and sleepy:
> "Bide yet! Bide a little!"
> The end of "yet" is far, however,
> And "bide a little" goes on forever. (120)

At the other extreme are poems so like Modern English that "translation" requires little change to anything but spelling—for instance, the beginning of "Adam lay bound":

Adam lay Ibowndyn
Bownden in a bond,
Fower thousand wynter
Thought he not to long. (111)

In every case I have tried to honor the original meaning, meter, and rhyme scheme while at the same time producing versions modern readers will enjoy. You can be confident in any of these poems that you are reading something close to the content, rhythm, and feeling of the original Middle English.

Of course no translation can match the real thing, or is meant to. For all my efforts, "Summer now is coming in" (1) sounds pallid beside the exuberant swing of "Svmer is icumen in." Even word-for-word modern equivalents lose the charm of Middle English spelling (though it is worth recalling that Middle English spelling probably held little charm for Middle English readers). For better or worse, "Between March and April" (3) will never be the same as "Bytuene mersh ant aueril."

Though reading Middle English poetry in its original language takes work, it is not as hard as it looks at first. You can get an idea of the difficulty from the original texts quoted here and from the catalog of first lines in Appendix B. If you enjoy these poems in translation, by all means look up the originals in the editions listed in the bibliography, and read them in Middle English. You will be glad you did.

NOTE ON ALLITERATIVE VERSE

The bulk of Middle English poetry is metrical, though sometimes only loosely so. As in much modern verse, its lines are constructed on patterns defined by stressed and unstressed syllables. For example, consider the line:

Yche DAY me CUMeþ TYDings THRE[3] (137)

Here, every other syllable is accented, or pronounced with more force than the one before it. An accented syllable following an unaccented syllable makes up an iambic foot. There are four iambs in the sample line, so its

_____

3. "Each day three worries come to me."

pattern is iambic tetrameter, a favorite meter of Middle English poets and later writers from Herrick to Auden.

Alliterative verse works on different principles. Predominant in the Old English period, this style of writing allows a varying number of syllables per line, but it requires that each line contain four accented syllables and that three of the four must alliterate, or share the same initial sound. Here is a line from the Old English epic *Beowulf,* probably written down around the year 1000:

Swa sceal GEong GUma   GODe geWYRcean[4]

The line has twelve syllables, but only four are accented and the first three of these alliterate. The words also break into two half-lines with a pause between them. All of this is typical of Old English poetry.

Although the Old English style of alliterative verse probably persisted in oral tradition, the Norman Conquest of 1066 marked its demise in written form until the fourteenth century, when it surfaced again in the Alliterative Revival, a literary movement noted for such superlative Middle English poems as *Gawain and the Green Knight* and *Piers Plowman.* By the fourteenth century the language was greatly changed, however, and Middle English poets adapted the Old English style freely. A good example is the fine alliterative poem *Saint Erkenwald* (p. 197), where four of the poem's first ten lines casually violate the classical pattern. The first line doesn't alliterate at all:

At LONdon in ENGlond nogt FULL long SYTHen.[5]

In line four every stressed syllable alliterates, not just the first three:

Saynt ERKenwolde as I HOPE þat HOly man HATte.[6]

Line seven has only one alliterating syllable in each half of the line:

---

4. "So should a young man work well."

5. "In London in England and not overlong."

6. "Saint Erkenwald, by my hope, was that holy man called." (Vowel sounds are considered to alliterate with each other and with the consonant *h*.)

For hit HEthen had BENE in HENGyst DAWes.[7]

And in line ten two alliterating units, the first syllable in *per*verted and the syllable *place,* are unaccented. Moreover, the *pl-* in *place* is not quite the same sound as the *p*'s in the other syllables:

And perVERtyd all þe PEpul þat in ÞAT place DWELLid.[8]

While not all Alliterative Revival work is as permissive as *Saint Erkenwald,* none of the Revival poets was a strict constructionist of the old style. Nevertheless, they created some striking poetry, often with a hard, Old English–flavored edge missing from more courtly work. Consider "In a forest as I fared . . ." (18), where the poet combines an unsentimental attitude with alliteration and a demanding rhyme scheme to unique effect. Other Alliterative Revival adaptations in this collection include the rowdy tour de force "Black, swarthy smiths . . ." (69) and the opening section of Langland's satire *Piers Plowman* (p. 124).

7. "For it had been heathen when Hengest ruled there."
8. "And perverted the people who lived in that place."

Worldly Lyrics

WORLDLY LYRICS

Although most surviving Middle English lyrics are religious, many of the best ones are secular, often exuberantly so. The appeal of these poems is strong and direct. Anyone can feel the promise of spring that bubbles through many of them or the anguish of suspicious or abandoned lovers. Other memorable impressions range from sweet apparent simplicity—for instance, in the radiant "Of every kind of tree" (4)—to the edgy insecurities of "I pray you, M . . ." (12).

This is not to say that the poems themselves are "natural" or unstudied. Many are influenced by established French themes and situations such as the *chanson d'aventure* (a man meets a maiden in the woods), the *chanson de jeune fille* (complaint of a young girl disappointed in love), and the *chanson de mal mariée* (condemning a bad marriage). Spring songs (or *reverdies*) were conventional too. Throughout the Middle English period and later, March 25, the feast of the Annunciation, was considered the start of the year, so April and May celebrate the beginning of a new year and recall Christ's conception as well. March, April, and May feature over and over in these lyrics. Riddles, seduction poems, and beast fables were also widely known forms. Even Middle English drinking songs and satires on women were rooted in Latin lyrics that students sang in Continental universities.

A good number of the poems here (and also in the "Religious Lyrics" section) are carols, songs like "I loved a lad and loved him free" (27) that begin with a *burden* or repeated element that then serves as a refrain after each stanza through the rest of the poem. These texts were probably meant to be sung, as were some other, less likely candidates such as "D . . . drunk—" (45), which is accompanied in its manuscript by a musical setting. The carols could very likely be danced to as well.

The poems show a wide range of styles and meters, reaching from the simple octosyllabic couplets found in "Go, little bill . . ." (8), to crossing rhyme and meter patterns with elaborate repeats as in "I'm always glad some mirth to make" (9), to the alliterative unrhymed verse of "Black, swarthy smiths . . ." (69). Middle English poets seem to have enjoyed intricate forms for their own sake. To see how demanding these could be, consider "In a forest as I fared . . ." (18), where alliterative lines are combined in a rhyming pattern that generally allows only two rhyme sounds over an eight-line stanza.

For all their conventional themes and formal elaboration, though, these lyrics project an appealing freshness, often set off by a bracing common sense that makes them recognizably English. Dealing with a lover's hopes, for example—a theme that could lead to a highly charged "courtly" supplication—the poem "Gracious and gay" (13) offers the obligatory despairing gesture ("To death I shall be brought"), but then immediately makes it clear that the lover has already been generously rewarded ("Ah, God, she's sweet beneath a sheet"), and ends with bold assurance, calling for another kiss.

Middle English poets and readers (or listeners) lived close to the earth and were sympathetic observers of the lives of birds and animals. They loved riddles, even easy ones such as "I have a new garden" (25) or "I have a young sister" (70), still a well-known folk song. Many of their poems tell or imply stories—for example, the Chaucer-like "Hogyn came to her bower's door" (22). Others are haunting and strange, like the apparent murder story in "Whenever there was in this town" (38) or the odd, languorous "At the north end of silver white" (66). Politics and English history crop up too, as in the Agincourt carol (62) or the lament for Edward III (63). Even the story of Robin and Gandelyn (58), a rare early ballad, has populist political overtones.

Considering the haphazard way these secular poems came down to us, it seems likely that a much greater number of comparable pieces have vanished. Today there are far more religious than secular Middle English poems, but that was probably not always the case. Of the forty-seven religious lyrics chosen for this book, for example, about half appear in more than one manuscript. Only eleven of the seventy-two secular lyrics and snatches do. This disparity alone shows us religious poems were copied more often in manuscripts (chiefly religious manuscripts) that had better prospects for being preserved, and therefore they had a stronger chance than secular poems to survive.

It appears likely, moreover, that the bulk of popular songs and poems were not written down to begin with. Some once-familiar Middle English lyrics are now known only by their titles, like the "Com hider, love, to me!" that Chaucer's Pardoner sings in *The Canterbury Tales*. In other cases, all that's left of a song is its burden or a few lines noted in a manuscript to recall the melody. Later writers often outfitted these familiar tunes with new words (usually a Latin religious text). At the time, everyone seems to have known such songs well enough for this shorthand to work reliably.

Of the secular poems that did get written down and managed to survive whole, a few appear in elaborate, beautifully produced collections like the British Library's Harley 2253 (the "Harley Lyrics"),[1] but most had a harder time of it. Many were written in the margins of other manuscripts or on odd leaves bound up with other texts. One great treasure—Bodleian Manuscript Rawlinson D. 913—is no more than a scribbled four-by-eleven-inch strip tucked into a mismatched volume of other manuscripts; and yet this scrap is our only link to several masterpieces such as "I am of Ireland" (83) and "All night beside the rose . . ." (2), which itself is probably a quatrain copied out of an otherwise lost longer poem. If pieces as memorable as these hang from so slender a thread, the loss of so many others must be regrettable indeed.

While the Harley Lyrics are largely sophisticated poems influenced by Continental styles, more commonplace Middle English lyrics and fragments are likely to appear in handbooks for preachers (who sometimes cited poems in their sermons), in commonplace books kept by individuals, or on blank pages and flyleaves of other manuscripts.

One source deserving special mention is the minstrel manuscript containing poems, and often musical notation as well, set down for the use of professional singers. By far the most important of these is British Library Manuscript Sloane 2593 (the "Sloane Lyrics"), our only source for such now-indispensable works as "I have a gentle cock" (14), "I have a young sister" (70), and "I sing of a maiden matchless" (125).

THE POEMS

1[2]

Summer now is coming in,
Loudly sing cuckoo!
Seeds grow and blossoms blow,

---

1. A facsimile of this manuscript is available: N. R. Ker, ed., *Facsimile of British Museum MS. Harley 2253*. Early English Text Society. London: Oxford UP, 1965. Individual pages can also be viewed at various Internet sites. Try a Google image search for "Harley 2253."

2. Appears with its music in a commonplace book kept at Reading Abbey.

And woods spring anew.
Sing cuckoo!

The ewe is bleating to her lamb.
The cows and calves low too.
The bullock starts; the wild buck farts.
Merrily sing cuckoo!
Cuckoo, cuckoo,
Come now and sing cuckoo.
Don't stop but sing it through!

Sing cuckoo now, cuckoo!
Sing cuckoo; sing cuckoo!

Index 3223. British Library, MS Harley 978. Musical setting. Thirteenth century. Unique.

2

All night beside the rose, the rose,
All night by the rose I lay.
I dared not steal the rose itself,
But bore the flower away.

Index 194. Bodleian, MS Rawlinson D. 913. Fourteenth century. Unique.

3

Between March and April,
When sweet sprays start to spring,
And small birds do their loving will,
As in their songs they sing,
I live in love and longing
For the fairest of all things.
What joy that girl could bring!
I'm hers alone, bound up, undone.

A happy hap has come to me.
I know it came by God's decree.

From other girls my love must flee,
And light on Alison.   *(refrain)*

Her hair is lovely, light, and fair,
Dark brows above the blackest eyes.
She laughs at me without a care.
Her little waist, ah, what a prize!
I swear unless the girl complies
And loves me back without disguise,
I'll bring about my own demise.
Ah, then my course is run.

Abed at night I twist and turn—
Tormented till my cheeks grow pale.
Yea, lady, this is your concern:
It's love that makes my spirit fail.
Of all the wisest men not one
Can sum up her I dote upon.
Her neck is whiter than the swan,
The fairest maiden in the town.

Now love has worn me down, alas,
Tossed like water to and fro,
Lest someone else might win the lass
Whom I have loved with such great woe.
But better suffer now, I know,
Than wait and suffer evermore.
Oh, fairest girl the world can show,
Hear my refrain and then I'm done.

Index 515. British Library, MS Harley 2253. Thirteenth century. Unique.

4

Of every kind of tree,
Of every kind of tree,
The hawthorn blossoms sweetest
Of every kind of tree.

My sweetheart she shall be,
My sweetheart she shall be,
The fairest thing that goes on earth,
My sweetheart she shall be.

Index 2622. Bodleian, MS Rawlinson D. 913. Fifteenth century. Unique.

5

Go, little ring, to that sweet maid
   Who holds my heart, as I admit.
Bow low. Beseech her to be swayed.
   Next pray that she will let you fit
   Her slender finger, touching it.
      Then tell her boldly—don't be shy:
      "My master wishes he were I."

Index 932. British Library, Royal MS 17.D.vi. Fifteenth century. Unique.

6

Bird on briar, bird, bird on briar!   *with a pun on* burde, *"girl"*
   We're born of love, and love we crave.
Have pity, bird, on my desire,
   Or make, dear love, make me my grave.

I am so bright, my bird on briar,
   To see that trim maid in the hall.
She's white of limb, all I admire;
   She's fair and true, the flower of all.

If I could have my will of her,
   Steadfast in love, lovely, true,
My woes would stop and never stir,
   For joy and bliss would make me new.

Index 521. King's College, Cambridge, Muniment Roll 2.W.32. Musical setting. Fourteenth
   century. Unique.

7

O Lord of Love, hear my complaint
　And do me right, as I require.
Why must I suffer in constraint?
　　What good is that? Must I expire?
　　Since you have set me in the fire
　　　　To burn my heart with ceaseless care,
　　Lord, bring me yet what I desire—
　　　　That fine, fresh maid who is so fair.

So fair she is, so fair and fresh,
　That all my love on her is set.　　　　　　　　　　10
She's best by far of face and flesh.
　　I've loved her long and love her yet;
　　A milder maid I never met.
　　　　Her countenance casts me in care;
　　The darling has me in her debt—
　　　　That fine, fresh maid who is so fair.

Of shining shapes I here commend
　Her upright stature, standing bright.
There's not a thing in her to mend;
　　Each part of her is fashioned right.　　　　　　　20
　　Whenever she is in my sight
　　　　No pain can make my heart forbear:
　　I'm hers alone, by love's great might—
　　　　That fine, fresh maid who is so fair.

Her feet, her hands, both soft and small,
　And every other piece of her,
Are each the comeliest of all.
　　I'd like to know each one, I'm sure.
　　I'm sick with love; she has the cure.
　　　　O let her listen to my prayer,　　　　　　　　30
　　Dispel my pains, make me secure—
　　　　That fine, fresh maid who is so fair.

When all her wonders fill my thought,
    I moan and sigh, call out, "Alas!"
In bitter bale thus am I brought,
    With pains I fear will never pass.
    In greater woe I never was.
        Unless she cures me of my care,
She'll be the death of me at last—
        That fine, fresh maid who is so fair.

Index 2491. British Library, Cotton Vespasian D. ix. Fourteenth century. Unique.

8

Mittitur: *"It is sent."*

Go, little bill, commend me heartily,   *little note*
To her I call my lady free.
Friday last, I bid you say,
She saw me when she went to pray.
I had a sparrow-hawk in hand.
Beside her stood my serving man.
An ancient woman sat by her,
Unmoving, pious, and demure.
Looking my way her face would soften—
I think—but say she glanced up often.
Another token I can send:
She came there with a pretty friend.
Behind the angle of the door
They knelt together on the floor.
I could hear them pitter-patter:
Their Matins . . . or some other matter!
Even then she looked at me,
Once or twice that I could see.
I left church early, quite discreet,
So I could meet them in the street.
Bid her read and picture me.
Commend me to her heartily!

Ringler Printed Index 474. Bodleian, Latin Misc. c.66. Sixteenth century. Unique.

9

I'm always glad some mirth to make,
If only for my lady's sake,
    When she sees me.
        But now I am away from her
    It may not be.

Though I must fare far from her sight,
I am her man both day and night.
    I'll never flee.
        But yet I wish as I love her
    She would love me.

When she is merry, I am glad.
When she is sorry, I am sad.
    The reason why?
        No man alive could treasure her
    As well as I.

She won't believe my love's so hot—
Says, "Seldom seen is soon forgot."
    It is not so.
        For by my faith save only her,
    I love no more.

Wherefore I pray both night and day
That she will cast all care away
    And come to rest;
        And evermore, no matter where,
    Love me the best.

And may I be as true to her,
Never changing nor unsure,
    Unto my last.
        I hope my love will never fail,
    But hold more fast.

Index 2381. Bodleian MS 6668. Musical setting. Fifteenth century. Unique.

10³

The smiling mouth and laughing eyes of gray,
  The long and slender arms and rounded breasts,
  Smooth hands, straight sides, and all the rest—
Your little feet . . . what can I further say?
I spend my time when you are far away
  Recalling you to quiet my unrest:
The smiling mouth and laughing eyes of gray,
  The long and slender arms and rounded breasts.
Permit me, dear, with no offense, I pray,
  To see you as I have in the past.
  No other sight on earth could be so blessed
Nor will be till the hour I pass away.
The smiling mouth and laughing eyes of gray,
  The long and slender arms and rounded breasts.

Index 3465. British Library, MS Harley 682. Fifteenth century. Unique.

11

My holy father, I confess,
  First to God and then to you,
  That at a window watched by few
I stole a sweet kiss and caress.
It was an impulse, I protest,
  But now it's done. What can I do?
My holy father, I confess,
  First to God and then to you.
  I'll give them back before I rest
To her, the girl I owe them to.
I'll see she has what she is due,
  Or tell me then that I transgress.
My holy father, I confess,
  First to God and then to you.

Index 2243. British Library, MS Harley 682. Fifteenth century. Unique.

3. This and the next poem are by Charles d'Orleans, who was taken prisoner at the Battle of Agincourt in 1415 and lived in England until his release in 1440. Both are rondels, a French form in which a line or set of lines is repeated three times.

12

I pray you, M, be true to me.
I'll be the same, as you will see.
I'll never change for old or new,
Nor love another—only you.
But you knew this from long ago;
I had your letter saying so.
I cherished every word you sent
And even more your sweet intent.
I had been sick the day before;
Your letter healed me. Sick no more!
M, in space
Come luck and grace.
I trust that's how all this will be
When good luck lights on you and me.
M, be steadfast—true in thought—
The sweetest love is dearest bought.
And M, my darling, you'll agree,
No one has paid as much as we.
Go as you will, where you may be
I'll come if you but call on me.
Therefore, dear, I pray, be true,
Or else my heart will split with rue.
Be steadfast, dear. I'm trusting you.
I'll never change for old or new.
Since we can't meet by other arts,
These writings must declare our hearts.

Ringler MS Index 677. Bodleian, Latin Misc. c.66. Sixteenth century. Unique.

13

Gracious and gay,
    On her lies all my thought.
Unless she pities me today,
    To death I shall be brought.

Her hands are fair as one could wish,
    Her arms are firm and round.

Her mouth is sweet as licorice—
    No finer can be found.

Her shining eyes are clear and gray,
    Her brows bend like a bow.
Her cheeks gleam like the rose in May,
    A slender waist below.

Ah, God, she's sweet beneath a sheet,
    I love no other so.
She'll always have my heart to keep,
    Wherever she may go.

Believe me now, my dear, I pray,
    My heart is yours, you know.
Kiss me, sweetheart, on my way,
    Once more before I go.

Index 1010. National Library of Ireland, D. 1435. Fifteenth century. Unique.

14

I have a gentle cock
    Who crows to me each day.
He bids me rise up early
    My Matins for to say.

I have a gentle cock.
    His lineage goes far back.
His comb is red as coral.
    His tail is deepest black.

I have a gentle cock.
    He comes from men of mark.
His comb is red as coral.
    His tail is full and dark.

His legs are purest azure,
    Small and slim to boot.

His spurs are white as silver,
   Down to their very root.

His eyes are made of crystal,
   Set in smoothest amber,
And every night he perches
   In my lady's chamber.

Index 1299. British Library, MS Sloane 2593. Fifteenth century. Unique.

15

Good day to you, dear Margaret.
All my love be with you yet.
I prize each sight of you I get—
In street, in chamber, "Ah, well-met!"
Our love's unknown to any man.
God grant we meet whenever we can!

Index 1121. Gonville and Caius College, Cambridge, MS 54. Fourteenth century. Unique.

16

"My death I love, my life I hate,
   And for a lady fair.
She is bright as noonday light,
   And that has caused my care.
Alas, I wither like the leaves
   Scorched by summer's glare.
For if my thought should help me naught,
   Where shall I turn my prayer?

"Sorrow, sighs, and dreary mind
   Bind my soul so fast   10
That I'll go mad and walk quite blind
   If I much longer last.
And yet my hurts with one sweet word
   She might at once recast.

What good is it, my lovely girl,
My hopes, my life, to blast?"

"Make off, you clerk, you are a fool!   cleric or student
I need say nothing more.
You'll never live beyond the day
You pass within my door.   20
If you're discovered in my room,
Your sorrows will be sore.
To trudge afoot may cause men grief,
But riding ill brings more."

"Alas, my dear! Why say such things?
Have pity on your man.
I swear you're always in my thought
In this or any land.
If I should die, dear, for your love,
You're shamed on every hand.   30
No! Let me live and be your love.
Dear, love me if you can."

"I called you fool and called you right!
Stop now and save your skin.
For you are watched both day and night
By father and my kin.
If you are taken in my bower,
They'll scarcely count it sin
Me to hold and you to slay.
Your death is all you'll win."   40

"Sweet lady, moderate your mood.
Relent and pity me.
I'm now a sad and wretched man
Who once went glad and free.
At a window, dear, we once,
Kissed fifty times, if three.

I swear to keep my longing hid.
Love, listen to my plea!"

"Wellaway! Now stop that talk!
My sorrows spring up new.   50
I loved a clerk, my paramour.
His love was strong and true.
He never went in bliss a day
Unless he saw me too.
I loved him better than my life.
Why should I lie to you?"

"My dear, while I was still at school,
You taught me love's sharp lore.
Ah, what I suffered for your love!
My wounds were deep and sore.   60
Far from home, away from men,
Upon the greenwood's floor,
Sweet lady, show you love me yet.
I'm done. I say no more."

"You're just the man to be a clerk.
Your voice is soft and still.
Well, you'll not suffer for my love
Love-pangs or other ill.
Father, mother, all my kin,
Can never hold me still.   70
I will be yours as you are mine.
You shall do all you will."

Index 2236. British Library, MS Harley 2253. Fourteenth century. Unique.

17

"I pray you come and kiss me,
My little, pretty Mopsy.
   I pray you come and kiss me."   *(burden)*

"Alas, good man, must you be kissed?
No, you shall not, on my bliss.
So go instead where you may list.
   I say you shall not kiss me."

"Consider, sweetheart. You must see
If you had asked much more of me,
I'd not hold back but soon agree.   10
   I pray you, come and kiss me."

"I grant you, sir, that you are kind
Where you may love and set your mind,
But words are often light, I find.
   And so you shall not kiss me."

"I only talk, dear, unrehearsed,
But you take all things for the worst."
"I do. So as I said at first,
   Indeed, you shall not kiss me."

"I pray you, let me kiss you.   20
But if I cannot kiss you,
Let me kiss your kerchief, do.
   I pray you, let me kiss you."

"I will be true to what I said.
Although you clamor to be fed,
My answer must suffice instead.
   Indeed, you shall·not kiss me"

"I see you hold your kisses dear.
If I should labor for a year,
I'd never gain an inch, I fear.   30
   Now then, come and kiss me."

"No, nor a half an inch indeed!
You will not break me, though you plead.

Wheedle, sir; you'll not succeed.
  Indeed, you shall not kiss me."

"I pray you come and kiss me,
My little, pretty Mopsy.
And if you will not kiss me,
  I pray you, let me kiss you."

"Well then you may; I will not stick.   40
But you must do no more than lick,
For if you think to clasp and prick,
  Indeed you shall not kiss me."

"Ah, now I see that you are kind.
If you could know my inmost mind,
I'm ever yours as you should find,
  And ready, dear, to kiss you."

Ringler MS Index 97. Canterbury Cathedral, Christ Church Letters ii.173. Sixteenth century. Unique.

18

In a forest as I fared without a friend,
Fortune found me the finest of fates—
A girl who glowed like the gold a man spends;
No girl could gleam with a grace more great.
"Who," I inquired, "are your kith and kin,
Kind maiden, so comely, so delicate?"
She bid me be silent then lest I offend;
My wooing and flattery wielded no weight.
"Hear me, heaven-sent creature," I hailed her.
"Don't think that I mean you the mildest of harms.   10
I'd far rather shield you from cares, all secure:
Comely, well clothed, and at peace in my arms."

"Clothes I have enough, and clean,
Garments that bring no chagrin.
Better poor raiment, lowly and lean

Than slide in thick robes, sink into sin.
Give you your wish and you'd grow less keen.
Once fed, I find men's thanks are thin.
Better discover now just what you mean
Than live to bewail what has been."   20

"Of bewailing, my lady, wail you no more.
My honor is yours, as is right.
My hand on this: till I'm old and hoar,
You are my love and my delight.
Why are you loath to believe my lore,
When my ardor has hit such a height?
Another might humbug you, girl, and implore
Without these promises I plight."

"Your precious promises I might rue
When pleasure, pride, and peace were gone.   30
You'd leave my love, take up a new,
Before the next nine nights were flown.
I'd hunger then for those I knew
But languish, hated and alone,
Despised by kith and kindred too,
Left begging for faith where faith had flown.

"Still, better a kind man in comely clothes,
Sir, in my arms to kiss and caress,
Than a bad, wretched husband, who, heaven knows,
Might throttle or thrash me, as all men attest.   40
My choicest choice here, as I suppose,
Is to let you embrace me and hope for the best,
Though I swore that I wouldn't with truth and oaths.
Our Lord leads us through life, as I guess.

"Fears for the future don't terrify me.
No wizard, I learn things by trial.
I'm a maid, and a meek one, sir, as you see.
Yet I'd welcome a man without guile."

Index 1449. British Library, MS Harley 2253. Fourteenth century. Unique.

19

We're wandering peddlers, light of foot,
The foul ways for to flee.   *(burden)*

We bear no stray cats' wretched skins
But purses, pearls, and silver pins,
Choice wimples shaped for ladies' chins.   *head coverings that surround the face*
   Damsel, buy some wares from me.

A pocket at my nether zone
Is shaped to hold two precious stones.
Damsel, had you tried them once,
   You'd be more apt to go with me.

I have a jelly by God's command.
It has no feet, but it can stand.
It can smite yet has no hand.
   Guess yourself what it may be.

I have a powder, too, to sell;
What it is I cannot tell.
It makes a maiden's womb to swell.
   Of this I have a quantity.

Index 3864. British Library, MS Sloane 2593. Fifteenth century. Unique.

20

A, a, a, a,
I love everywhere I go.   *(burden)*

In all this world's no merrier life
Than a young man leads without a wife.
He lives at ease and free of strife,
   In every place that he may go.

In every place he's first of all
Among the maidens, great and small,

In dancing, piping, playing ball,
  In every place that he may go.

Lasses who scorn married men
When these play at ball for them
Dote on young lads even then,
  In every place that they may go.

Then maidens say, "Ah, farewell Jack!
Your love goes with you, like your pack.
You bear your love upon your back,
  In every place that you may go."

Index 1468. Bodleian MS 29734. Fifteenth century. Unique.

21

O mistress, why
Outcast am I
To mourn and cry
  Away from you?
Since you and I,
Unless I lie,
Have by the by
  Had much ado?

All lovingly
You came to me
Sans company
  To bless my hopes.
But now I see
Discourteously
You sentence me
  To lurk and mope.

For now apart
You wring my heart.
You make me smart
  By this cruel ploy.

Your pride, my dame,
Might blot with shame
The duchess's name
    Of high Savoy.

You must agree
That since you're free
To look past me
    And not to speak,
It fits my case
To seek for grace
Some other place—
    And be less meek.

Ringler MS Index 1206. British Library, MS Harley 2252. Sixteenth century. Unique.

22

Hogyn came to her bower's door,
Hogyn came to her bower's door,
And rattled the latch for love.
    Hum, ha, trill, go bell—
And rattled the latch for love.
    Hum, ha, trill, go bell.

Up she rose, and let him in,
Up she rose, and let him in,
She meant to honor all her kin.   *sarcasm*
    Hum, ha, trill, go bell—   10
She meant to honor all her kin.
    Hum, ha, trill, go bell.

Yet when the two were snug in bed,
Yet when the two were snug in bed,
He could do nothing, on my head.
    Hum, ha, trill, go bell—
He could do nothing, on my head.
    Hum, ha, trill, go bell.

"Go outside my window there,
Go outside my window there,
And I will come to you, I swear."   20
    Hum, ha, trill, go bell—
"And I will come to you, I swear."
    Hum, ha, trill, go bell.

He went outside. "I'm here," he hissed.
He went outside. "I'm here," he hissed.
She turned out her ass for him to kiss.
    Hum, ha, trill, go bell—
She turned out her ass for him to kiss.
    Hum, ha, trill, go bell.   30

"Alas, my dear, you do me wrong,
Alas, my dear, you do me wrong,
Or else your breath is wondrous strong!"
    Hum, ha, trill, go bell—
"Or else your breath is wondrous strong!"
    Hum, ha, trill, go bell.

Ringler MS Index 601. Balliol College, Oxford, MS 354. Sixteenth century. Unique.

23

Spring has come with love to town
With blooms and birds and pleasant rounds
    And other blissful things.
Daises shine along the dales,
The sweet notes of the nightingales—
    Each bird takes heart and sings.
The thrushes rouse and threaten so;
Forgotten is their winter woe,
    When the woodruff springs.
Birds' voices rise up everywhere,   10
Self-satisfied and debonair,
    So all the forest rings.

The rose bursts forth from her green hood.
The leaves among the shining wood
   Keep their appointed time.
The moon spreads out her silver light.
The lily sweetens our delight,
   With fennel and with thyme.
Wild drakes go wooing soon and late.
All animals have found their mates   20
   Like streams that merge and chime.
But moody men grouch and condemn.
I know, for I am one of them,
   Unsettled by love's crimes.

The moon, I say, pours out her light;
So does the sun, but far more bright;
   The birds sing as they should.
Soft dews dampen all the downs;
Creatures murmur secret sounds
   Not quickly understood.   30
The worms are coupling in the earth,
And yet girls swell with their own worth—
   They think themselves so good.
If I can't win the will of one
Let joy go hang! I vow I'll run
   An outlaw in the wood.

Index 1861. British Library, MS Harley 2253. Thirteenth century. Unique.

24

Fowls in the forest,
Fishes in the foam,
Yet I grow mad and moan.
I walk with sorrow in my breast
For best of blood and bone.   *with a pun on "beast"*

Index 864. Bodleian MS 21713. Musical setting. Thirteenth century. Unique.

25

I have a new garden,
    One that's new begun.
There's not another garden
    Like mine beneath the sun.

In the center of my garden
    A pear tree has been set.
It bears no other burden
    But pretty pears Jennet.   *pears of Jean, an early variety*

The fairest maid in town
    Came here and begged of me
To have a shoot or graft
    Of my stout, fruitful tree.

I gave her what she asked,
    And just as she designed,
She filled me up in turn
    With heady ale and wine.

I made the graft, indeed,
    Right up in her home,
And then for weeks and months
    It flourished in her womb.

A year from that same day
    The lady and I met.
She said it was per Robert,   *by Robert (the speaker's name)*
    And never per Jennet!

Index 1302. British Library, MS Sloane 2593. Fifteenth century. Unique.

26

Would to God that it were so,
As I would wish, between us two.   *(burden)*

The man I love, and love the best
    In all this country, east or west,
Repays me strangely, I profess.
    Why wonder that I go in woe?

When I most wish that he would stay,
    He makes great haste to go.
No farewell, good-bye, good day.
    Why should he treat me so?

In many places when we meet
    I dare not speak, but forth I go.
With heart and eyes that man I greet,
    So much in love I know no more.

And as he is my heart's true love,
    My dearest dear, blessed may he be,
I firmly swear by God above
    None has my love but only he.

I'm comforted on every side,
    All colors shine forth fresh and new,
When he is come and will abide.
    I know well then that he is true.

I love him dearly, no one else.
    I would to God he knew!
Ah, if he loved me half as well,
    I'd turn to no one new.

Index 3418. Cambridge University, Additional MSS 5943. Fifteenth century. Unique.

27

If what is done were yet undone,
I would be wary.   *(burden)*

I loved a lad and loved him free.
I thought he felt the same for me.

Now I myself the truth can see,
    That he is far.

He promised to be kind and true
And never change for someone new.
Now I am sick and pale of hue,
    For he is far.

He said he'd never do me ill,
And so I let him have his will.
Now I am sick and mourning still,
    For he is far.

Index 1330. Gonville and Caius College, Cambridge, MS 383. Fifteenth century. Unique.

28

I am old, and age can bite.
My young wife flits and puts me by.
Many a young girl roves at night,
Whoring herself. I'll tell you why:
I can't do my office, though I try.
So I'm betrayed. Old age is dry.
The young don't care; they cheat and lie.
Blind men like me eat many a fly.

Ringler MS Index 630. Bodleian MS 10234. Sixteenth century. Unique.

29

To my love, as moist as chalk,
And stable as a weathercock,
This letter.   *(burden)*

To you, you brabbler, I must write.
You've caused me enough of despair.
Your virtues are more than a maid can recite.
To say less than that is unfair.
Your looks are perfect—passing fair,

Graceful, handsome as an owl,
The comeliest of any fowl!

Your foremost features, I declare,
Your brow, your mouth, your nose so flat,
Would look as well upon a hare,   10
And maybe better on a cat!
I'd say much more if I knew what.
Curse your face and curse your guts!
Curse your whoring and your sluts!

Yet I should praise your manly build,
From shoulders down, before, behind.
No artist, no, however skilled,
Could shape a worse build in his mind.
(Keep patience, sir, though you're maligned.)
Your rumpled garments hang and cling   20
Like a goose that drags a broken wing.

Your thighs are mangled, shanks much worse;
Your knees turn out as if you rowed
Or each one feared the other's curse.
Ah, such ill legs, all gnarled and bowed;
I swear they would disgrace a toad!
Beneath these are your stunted heels,
Dry and split like apple peels!

She who loved so sweet a man
Might well be glad that she was born.   30
She who used the dark to span
And prick herself upon your thorn—
She might as well be hanged at morn
Who with two eyes chose such a troll,
And for your sake held up her hole!

I rip your love with bloody nails.
May lice eat you and all such males!

Ringler MS Index 1760. Bodleian MS 14530. Fifteenth century. Unique.

30

Hey nonny! Hey nonny!
I love Sir John, if I love any!   *(burden)*

O Lord, so sweet Sir John does kiss,
   Every time that we would play,
No other man so pleasant is.
   I have no power to say him nay.

Sir John loves me and I love him,
   And will forever if I may.
He says, "Sweetheart, come kiss me trim."
   I have no power to say him nay.

Sir John is kind: he never mocks.
   He takes his pleasure and he pays.
He puts his offering in my box.
   I have no power to say him nay.

When Sir John's mouse is in my trap,
   I'd keep him there both night and day.
He gropes so well about my lap,
   I have no power to say him nay.

Sir John gives me shiny rings
   And other presents bright and gay—
The sleekest furs and other things.
   I have no power to say him nay!

Index 2494. Huntington Library MS EL 1160. Fifteenth century. Unique.

31

"Kyrie" and "Kyrie"   *Kyrie eleison, "Lord, have mercy,"*
Our Jenkin sings so merrily,   *a refrain sung early in the Mass*
With "aleison." [4]   *(burden)*

   4. The references in the poem track the unfolding of the Latin Mass, from the *Kyrie* at the beginning to *Deo Gracias,* the congregation's last response before the Mass ends. "Aleison" in the burden may hint that the speaker's name is Alison.

As I went in our Yule procession,
I knew pert Jenkin by his tone:
  Kyrie eleison.

Amid the music for that day,
It did me good to hear him say,
  "Kyrie eleison."

He read the epistle fair and well.
It did me good, and ever shall:
  Kyrie eleison.

He trilled the *Sanctus* like a bird.
That did me good, upon my word:
  Kyrie eleison.

His notes danced gaily, as they ought,
Like small peas boiling in a pot:
  Kyrie eleison.

Singing the *Agnus* like a flute,   *"Lamb [of God]"*
He winked and tread upon my foot:
  Kyrie eleison.

Benedicamus Domino; Christ be mild.   *"Bless the Lord."*
And *Deo gracias;* I go with child!   *"Thanks be to God."*
  Kyrie eleison.

Index 377. British Library, MS Sloane 2593. Fifteenth century. Unique.

32

When the nightingale sings
  And woods break out green,
When leaves and grass and blossoms spring—
  In April, I mean—
When love has deep inside my heart
  Thrust its spear so keen,

So night and day it drinks my blood,
  My life decays unseen.

I've loved so hot this year
  That I may love no more.   10
I have sighed my fill of sighs,
  O sweetheart I adore,
And still your love seems far away.
  This wrings my heart full sore.
Sweetest maid, reward my love;
  It's yours as heretofore.

Sweetheart dear, I pray from you,
  Just one loving speech.
Though I walk the world so wide
  No other will I seek.   20
With your love, my darling one,
  My bliss can but increase.
A single kiss from your sweet mouth,
  I swear, would be my leech.   *doctor*

Sweetheart dear, I pray from you
  Some sign your love is keen.
So if you love me, as you may,
  Show it by your mien.
Dear, if your will inclines my way,
  Now let your love be seen.   30
In truth, I think on you so much
  For love I'm turning green.

From Lincoln to Lindsey, as I say,
  Northampton up to Lound,   *towns in the East Midlands*
I've never seen so fair a maid.
  Your beauty has me bound.
Sweetheart dear, I pray that you
  With love will see me crowned,
Or I must moan my loving song
  To you who are love's ground.   40

Index 4037. British Library, MS Harley 2253. Fourteenth century. Unique.

33

My cares are always springing new.
　　Dear God! This time no help there is,
For I am judged and held untrue,
　　All guiltless, as I hope for bliss.

My faith's proved good in any place
　　Or any course that I pursue.
I've won men's trust, by God's great grace.
　　But now there's nothing I can do.

Index 2231. Bodleian MS 21956. Musical setting. Fourteenth century. Unique.

34[5]

O kindly creature of beauty peerless,
Glorious mirror of all clearness,
Some sign of love, I pray with humbleness,
Show your servant in great distress.

Index 2475. Bodleian MS 6668. Musical setting. Fifteenth century. Unique.

35

Go, heart, hurt with adversity,
　　Let my lady thy wounds see,
And tell her this, as I tell thee:
　　"Farewell joy and welcome pain,
　　Until I see her face again."

Index 925. Bodleian MS 6668. Musical setting. Fifteenth century. Unique.

36[6]

My love has gone to other lands.
　　Alas, why has she so?

　　5. This poem is a brief example of the "aureate" style of the later fifteenth century. Poets searched for the most "golden," or artificial, way to say things, usually turning to stilted Latinate diction. In longer works the effect can be numbing.
　　6. This may be the song Chauntecleer sings in "The Nun's Priest's Tale."

And I'm bound here in love's strong bands.
　Her leaving is my woe.
　　She has my very heart to hold
　　Wherever she may ride or go,
　With love a thousandfold!

Index 2254. Trinity College, Cambridge, MS 599. Fourteenth century. Unique.

37

This is no life that I have led,
　But death, alas, though in life's likeness
With endless sorrow, full of dread,
　Beyond despair, devoid of gladness.
　I have no help in all this sadness—
　　Nothing to ease me or amend
　　Till death shall come to make my end.

Index 3613. Cambridge University, Folio MS I.6. Fifteenth century. Unique.

38

Whenever there was in this town
　Ale or wine,
I would buy it gladly
　For that dear love of mine.
That man was right hardy
　Who left her lying bloody.
If he were the king's son
　Of Normandy,
Yet I would avenge
　That dear love of mine.
Lord God, I was filled with woe.
　I was filled with woe.
When a man loses what he loves,
　It's always so.
Neither earl nor lord . . .
　No! Not another line!

I pray she rests above with Christ,
    That dear love of mine.

Index 3898. Bodleian, MS Rawlinson D. 913. Fourteenth century. Unique.

39[7]

When winter nettles bear roses red,
    And twining thorns wear figs,
And bushes burst with loaves of bread
    And cherries on each twig,
    And oaks are hung with pears and pigs,
        And honey comes from leeks . . .
        Trust women and be meek.

When sardines chase tall stags through trees,
    And herrings blow their horns,
And trout bounce grouse upon their knees,
    And cods shoot springing corn,
    And geese course wolves through frost at morn,
        And smelts discourse in Greek . . .
        Trust women and be meek.

When sparrows raise steeples to the sky,
    And wrens haul grain in sacks,
And curlews rub wet horses dry,
    And seagulls oil their tack,
    And doves wear hunting knives and quack,
        And griffins bow and molt their beaks . . .
        Trust women and be meek.

When crabs catch woodcocks in the parks,
    And hares crack snails to eat,
And camels set snares to capture larks,
    And field mice winnow wheat,
    And ducks kiss relics in the street,

7. This poem uses a version of rhyme royal, a stanza Chaucer introduced into English.

And shrewd wives turn the other cheek,
Trust women and be meek.

Index 3999. Balliol College, Oxford, MS 354. Fifteenth century. Not unique.

40

Of creatures, women are the best.
Cuius contrarium verum est.[8]   *"The opposite of this is true." (burden)*

In every place a man may see
Women true as doves in trees,
Not loose of lip, all must agree:
A mighty joy to every he.

Women are steadfast as the sun,
So gentle, so courteous, every one,
Meek as lambs, still as stone—
Crooked or crabby, there are none!

Men are far more rough and cruel.
I hold that no one but a fool   10
Rebels against a woman's rule.
They are so patient, calm, and cool.

Sirs, tell a woman all you will
And she will keep it wondrous well.
She'd rather go alive to hell,
Than find another wife to tell.

Through women men are reconciled.
Through women no man is beguiled.
Griselda-like although reviled,   *Chaucer's patient heroine*
In every trial they're meek and mild.   20

8. Part of the joke may have been that women weren't expected to know Latin. Chaucer plays the same trick in "The Nun's Priest's Tale" by having Chauntecleer explain to his wife that "*mulier est hominis confusio*" (woman is a man's ruination) means "womman is mannes joye."

(You must agree, or else be still.)
They won't displease us by their will.
At angry words they have no skill.
Their minds are never apt for ill.

Who can say they love to natter,
Betray their husbands' faults with chatter?
They'd rather fast on bread and water
Than lay us bare through idle clatter.

If all long-suffering were drowned,
So none was left on sea or ground,   30
Some yet could be in women found,
So greatly does their worth abound!

To the tavern wives won't go,
Nor to the alehouse, as you know.
By God, their hearts would split with woe
To waste their husbands' money so.

Suppose you saw a wife today,
Who loved fine clothes and rich array,
Sumptuous kerchiefs, great display.
She isn't proud for all you say.   40

Index 1485. Balliol College, Oxford, MS 354. Fifteenth century. Not unique.

41

How! Hey! There's no release.
I dare not speak when she says, "Peace!"   *(burden)*

Young men, listen, every one,
Tough, old women, take you none.
I have such a wife at home.
I dare not speak when she says, "Peace!"

When I come from the plow at noon,
My dish is cracked, the loaf rough-hewn.
Afraid to ask my dame a spoon,
I dare not speak when she says, "Peace!"

If I ask my dame for bread,
She takes a staff and breaks my head.
I hide myself beneath the bed!
I dare not speak when she says, "Peace!"

If I ask my dame for meat,
She throws the dish down at my feet,
With "You're not worth a shriveled beet!"
I dare not speak when she says, "Peace!"

If I ask my dame for cheese,
"Boy," she answers, if you please,
"You're not worth a cup of peas!"
I dare not speak when she says, "Peace!"

Index 4279. British Library, MS Sloane 2593. Fifteenth century. Unique.

42

I am quick as any deer
In praise of women, as you may hear.   *(burden)*

To dispraise women were a shame
For, sirs, a woman was your dame.   *mother*
Our Blessed Lady was the same—
A woman, named and fashioned so.

A woman is a worthy thing,
Glad to wash and glad to wring.
"Lullaby, sweetheart," she doth sing,
Yet all she has is care and woe.

A woman shines to all men's sight:
She serves a man both day and night,
And serves him, sirs, with all her might.
Yet all she has is care and woe.

Index 3782. British Library, MS Harley 4294. Sixteenth century. Unique.

43

Care get away, away;
Mourning get away.
I am forsaken;
Another is taken.
I dry my tears today!   *(burden)*

I am sorry for her sake,
Yet I will eat and drink.
Better sleep full sound than wake
And sit and sigh and think.

I am swamped by care and fear
And cast in such decline,
That when I rise up from my bed,
My first thought is to dine.

I am cast in such decline,
So swamped by care and fear,
When I can drink my fill of wine,
I never think of beer.

Index 1280. Gonville and Caius College, Cambridge, MS 383. Fifteenth century. Unique.

44

Bring us in good ale, and bring us in good ale.
For Our Blessed Lady's sake, now bring us in good ale!   *(burden)*

Bring us in no brown bread, for that is made of bran.
Bring us in no white bread; white bread shall be banned.
Yea, bring us in good ale!

Bring us in no beef, for beef has many bones.
But bring us in good ale, for that goes down at once.
Yea, bring us in good ale!

Bring us in no bacon, for that is passing fat.
But bring us in good ale; we're keen enough for that!
Yea, bring us in good ale!

Bring us in no mutton, for that is often lean.
Nor bring us in no tripes, for tripes are seldom clean.
Nay, bring us in good ale!

Bring us in no eggs, for eggs are full of shells.
But bring us in good ale, and give us nothing else.
Yea, bring us in good ale!

Bring us in no butter; therein are many hairs.
Nor bring us in no pig's flesh; that's only fit for bears.
Nay, bring us in good ale!

Bring us in no chickens; they're costly to acquire.
Nor bring us in no ducks; ducks dabble in the mire.
Nay, bring us in good ale!

Index 549. Bodleian MS 29734. Musical setting. Fifteenth century. Not unique.

45

D . . . drunk—
    Drunken, drunken, drunk—
    Drunk is Tabard on wine.   *speaker's name*
Hey, Sister, Walter, Peter . . .
    You've drained a pail.
    Now I'll not fail!

Let everything stand still—
   Still and still and still.
Let everything stand still—
   Still as any stone.
Trip a little with your foot,
   By God, you're overthrown!

Index 694.11. Bodleian, MS Rawlinson D. 913. Musical setting. Fourteenth century. Unique.

46

Omnes gentes plaudite.   *"Everyone applaud."*
I saw some blackbirds in a tree.
They took their flight and flew away,
With *ego dixi,* sirs, good day.   *"I say."*
Many white feathers has a magpie—[9]
I can't sing more; my lips are dry!
Many white feathers has the swan—
I've drunk so much the words are gone!
Feed the fire and make it blaze.
One more drink, then take our ways.

Index 2675. British Library, MS Sloane 2593. Fifteenth century. Unique.

47

I tell you, Anna Taylor, dame,
We're lacking drink, and you're to blame.
Look here, dame, unbar your door.
Let us in to drink some more!

Madam, though we're far in debt
For all the good wine we have got,
In for a little, in for a lot!
I drank before and would drink yet.

Ringler MS Index 826. British Library, Additional MSS 14997. Circa 1500. Unique.

9. Literally true, but it has more black ones.

48[10]

A king, I sit and look about.
Tomorrow I may go without.

Woe is me, my kingship's past.
I flourished till I fell, alas.

I was rich not long ago;
Now I'm made poor by fortune's blow.

I shall be king, as men will see,
When this wretch's death makes room for me.

Index 1822. British Library, MS Harley 7322. Fourteenth century. Not unique.

49

Lords, England's in a sorry state:
We love ourselves and conscience hate;
Many knights but little might;
Many laws but little right;
Many acts of Parliament,
Yet few put forth with true intent;
Small charity but smiling faces;
Bankrupt gallants feigning graces;
Much peculation; much disguising;
Much recklessness and misadvising;
Great expense but little wages;
Countless gentles, fewer pages;
Heavy gowns with ample sleeves;
Highly placed and shameless thieves.
Most are anxious for their clothes,
But not their tongues; they dirty those.

Index 2335. Corpus Christi College, Oxford, MS 237. Fifteenth century. Not unique.

10. Each couplet would be suitable to identify a character at a different position on a wheel of fortune.

50[11]

Trusty. Seldom to their friends unjust.
   Glad to help. No Christian creature
Willing to grieve. Setting all their joy and lust
   Only in pleasuring of God. Having no care
   Who is most rich. With them they will be severe.
      Where need is never giving alms away
      Without reason. Thus are priests, I say.

Trusty seldom. To their friends unjust.
   Glad to help no Christian creature.
Willing to grieve. Setting all their joy and lust
Only in pleasuring. Of God having no care.
   Who is most rich, with them they will be. Severe
      Where need is. Never giving alms away.
      Without reason. Thus are priests, I say.

Ringler MS Index 1776. Pembroke College, Cambridge, MS 307. Sixteenth century. Unique.

51

I hold him wise and rightly taught
Who bears a horn, but blows it not.   *(burden)*

Blowing fits the greatest game.
Blow for less, and bear the blame.
And so I hardly hold it shame
   To bear a horn, but blow it not.

Horns can sound forth loud and shrill.
When you should blow, sirs, blow your fill,
But when you shouldn't, hold you still,
   And bear your horn, but blow it not.

Whatsoever be your thought,
Watch and listen, saying naught,

11. A "punctuation poem." Rearranging the periods makes all the difference.

And then shall men say you are taught
   To bear a horn, but blow it not.

Of helpful saws beneath the sun,
Sirs, this is the topmost one:
"Hold your peace, and loose talk shun.
     Yea, bear a horn, but blow it not."

Whatever swells within your breast,
Stop your mouth up with your fist.
Wait. Think of "*Had I guessed!*"
   And bear a horn, but blow it not.

And when you sit before your ale,
Singing like a nightingale,
Beware to whom you tell your tale.
   Best bear a horn, but blow it not.

Index 543. Bodleian MS 29734. Fifteenth century. Unique.

52[12]

A fool myself, my work is bad.
Take me up, I hold you mad.
I burn hot. I smite sore.
Take me up and thrive no more.
Dreadful deaths from me have sprung.
   I am a well of woe.
I've slain great monarchs, fair and strong.
   And I shall slay more.

Index 1269. British Library, MS Harley 7322. Fourteenth century. Unique.

53

Alas, what should we friars[13] do
Now common men know holy writ?

12. A riddle. The answer may be "love," or "wrath" or "ambition."

13. Members of religious begging orders who went about preaching instead of living in monasteries.

All about where I may go
They boldly cross my will with it.

I wonder how it could be so.
What evil sharpened humdrum wits?
Certainly we'll sink full low
Unless we somehow pay them quits.

I think the Devil is to blame—
To cast the gospel in our tongue!   10
Now simple men are lost to shame;
Their stony hearts cannot be wrung!

When I come into a shop
With "*in principio,*"   *"in the beginning [was the word],"*
They greet my words with "Friar, hop!   *conventional friars' greeting*
Go sweat to win your silver. Go!"

If I reply it isn't fit
For priests to work like other men,
They draw a page from holy writ
With, "What did good Saint Paul do then?"   20

They touch the habit on my back
And say, "In truth, upon our oaths,
Whether brown or white or black,   *colors worn by various orders*
That's worth the sum of all our clothes!"

I say, "I beg here not for me,
But those whom fortune has undone."
They say, "You've got your two or three,
Give those you're so concerned for one."

Thus our deceits have been found out
By men like these and many more.   30
No longer welcome round about,
We're passed along from door to door.

Should this go on, the outlook's dire.
Our order and our claims disgraced,

Men shall hardly find a friar
In England in a little space.

Index 161. St. John's College, Cambridge, MS 195. Fifteenth century. Unique.

54

Deceit deceives and shall be deceived,
   For by deception we all may be grieved.
Although his own lies go unperceived,
   Lies told to a liar may be believed.
   Fraud quit with fraud is rightly achieved,
     For fraudulent is soon fraudulent found.
     To every defrauder fraud always rebounds.

Index 674. Bodleian MS 4119. Fourteenth century. Not unique.

55[14]

Deceit puts on a trusty show,
   Double as fortune, turning like a ball,
But brittle at need as a rotten bow.
   Who lives by trust is ripe to fall.
   Good friend or ill, there's guile in all.
   When want is great, faith may be small.
     So beware of trust, as I advise.
     Trust to yourself and learn to be wise.

Index 145. Bodleian MS 1486. Fourteenth century. Unique.

56[15]

It's merry while the summer lasts,
Alive with birds and song;
But now we feel the cold wind's blast
And weather strong.

---

14. This is a flyleaf poem, one jotted on the opening page of another manuscript.
15. Another flyleaf poem.

Aiee, Aiee, this night is long,
And I in pain must suffer wrong,
And sorrow, mourn, and fast.

Index 2163. Bodleian MS 14755. Musical setting. Thirteenth century. Unique.

57[16]

As I went out to take the air,
    Walking in the fields alone,
I heard the mourning of a hare.
    Full ruefully he made his moan:

"Alas! Dear God, I'm badly placed,
    Attacked on every hand.
From dale to down each day I'm chased—
    I may not sit or stand!

"I swear I neither rest or sleep.
    No valley is secure.   10
No brush or thicket may me keep;
    No hiding place is sure.

"Hunters will not stay for Mass,
    Such pleasure hunting yields.
They yoke their eager hounds, alas,
    And lead them to the field.

"Their dogs run in from every side
    To pin me in a furrow.
The masters spur their mounts and ride,
    Hallooing as they go.   20

16. This and the next poem are ballads, a popular storytelling form with a characteristic alternation of four-beat and three-beat lines. Many of the traditional ballads we know today probably originated in the Middle English period as oral poetry but were not written out or printed until much later. This one is typical in its conventional opening, stock characterization, and ultimately resigned air. See also "Good Saint Steven was a clerk" (116).

"Soon they're closing on my hide.   *lair*
  I crouch and sit full low.
A moment more and I am spied.
  'So ho!' rings out. 'So ho!'

" 'Ha,' says one, 'there sits a hare—
  Rise up, Wat! Halloo!'   *traditional hare's name*
And then to save my life, I swear,
  That's just what I must do!

"In winter when the snow spreads round
  I'm easier to trace.   30
My prints lie waiting to be found.
  Once found, next comes the chase.

"When I creep into towns or farms
  To eat the greens or leeks,
The village dogs raise loud alarms
  And chase me till I'm weak.

"Or if I sit and crop the kale
  And the wife is in the way,
She runs out roaring like a gale:
  'I'll kill him if I may!'   40

" 'Scat!' she calls, 'get out, you knave,'
  And strides along the row.
I see she bears a wooden stave
  To slay me at a blow.

" 'Leave that, by God, you thievish Wat!
  My life, sir, you shall die.
I have a snare. It's strong and taut.
  You'll feel it by and by.'

"And then the shrew calls out her hounds,
  And sets them on my trail.   50

They chivy me about the grounds.
   'Go dogs! Run hard!' she rails.

"In fields or towns, that's how things go.
   I never can rest safe.
God knows my life is full of woe.
   I bump from scrape to scrape.

"There is no beast upon the land,
   No buck or doe, I swear,
That's so abused on every hand
   As is a simple hare.   60

"If a gentleman comes seeking sport
   And finds me in my den,
For fear of scorn and ill report
   He will not kill me then.

"An acre's breadth he will allow
   Before he slips his hounds.
Of every kind of man, I vow,
   May gentlemen abound!

"Once spotted, though, I'm easy prey:
   The greyhounds catch me quick.   70
Split open, entrails cast away,
   I'm brought home on a stick.

"Next I'm left to age a while,
   Hanging from a pin.
With leeks and herbs I'm served in style.
   Their whelps play with my skin."

Index 559. National Library of Wales, MS Porkington 10. Fifteenth century. Not unique.

58

I heard this telling of a clerk,
   Down by yon wood's side,

Of Robin Hood and Gandelyn.
   It's true, unless he lied.

Those two were never common thieves,
   But bowmen and fast friends.
They roved the woods to hunt for meat
   And take what good God sends.

All day they went, those two bold men,
   But quarry found they none,   10
Until at last the evening came,
   And Robin would go home.

Half a hundred fine, fat deer
   Just then they came upon,
And every one was sleek and fit
   Beneath the slanting sun.
"By God I swear," said Robin Hood,
   "We'll have the choicest one!"

Robin bent his jolly bow.
   Therein he set a shaft.   20
The fattest deer of all the herd,
   He split its heart in half.

He hadn't skinned the fallen deer
   Halfway from its hide
When an arrow winging from the west
   Felled Robin in his pride.
Gandelyn crouched down full low
   And peered from side to side.

"O who has slain my lord?" he said.
   "Who did this evil deed?   30
I'll never from this greenwood go,
   Until I've seen him bleed."

Gandelyn looked from east to west
   And peered beneath the sun.
At last he saw another youth—
   Wrennok, he was, of Donne.

A bow was in this Wrennok's hand,
   An arrow set therein,
With four-and-twenty other shafts
   Well trussed up in a skin.   40
"Beware," he said, "now, Gandelyn,
   Or taste that arrow's twin.

"Beware, beware, now, Gandelyn,
   Or you'll have one of these."
"A shot apiece," said Gandelyn,
   "And woe to him who flees."

"Say, what's the mark that we must hit?"
   Said this Gandelyn.
"Shoot till someone's heart is split,"
   The other answered him.   50

"And who shall be the first to shoot?"
   Said young Gandelyn.
"Let me try a shot at you"—
   Thus Wrennok hoped to win.

Wrennok loosed a full good shot,
   Rather low than high.
It made its way through Gandelyn's breeks,   *breeches*
   But never touched his thigh.

"Ah, now you've had your chance at me,"
   Gandelyn called out,   60
"But if Our Lady's on my side,
   I'll see you paid, no doubt."

With that the young man bent his bow
   And set therein a shaft.
It flew through Wrennok's shirt of green
   And cut his heart in half.

"Now, Wrennok, you shall never brag,
   At ale, nor yet at wine,
That you have slain both Robin Hood
   And his man Gandelyn.   70

"No, Wrennok, you've no call to brag
   At wine, nor yet at ale.
When Robin fell before your bow,
   That Gandelyn proved frail."

Index 1317. British Library, MS Sloane 2593. Fifteenth century. Unique.

59

"Pax vobiscum," said the fox,   *"Peace be with you."*
"For I am come to town."   *(burden)*

It happened in the dark of night,
The fox fell to with all his might,
Without a coal or candlelight,
   When he came into town.

When he reached the farmer's yard,
The farmer's geese were on their guard.
"Oh, geese," he said, "I'll use you hard,
   Before I leave the town."

He skulked beside the farmer's house,
Creeping softly as a mouse;
He feared the farmer and his spouse,
   When he was in the town.

He snatched the first goose he could spy.
Lord, how the geese began to cry!
Out swarmed the men with "Hey!" and "Hie!"
    And called, "Fox, put her down!"

"No!" he said, with wicked glee;
"She goes into the wood with me,
Until we stop beneath a tree,
    Among the berries brown.

"I have a wife, but she is sick,
And many babies tumbling thick.
Those babies want some bones to pick
    Before they will lie down."

Index 1622. British Library, Royal 19.B.iv. Fifteenth century. Unique.

60

Make we merry, rich and poor,
Christmastime has come once more.   *(burden)*

Let no man come into this hall,
Haughty knight or humble thrall,
Unless some sport he bring withal,
For now's the time of Christmas.

If he says he cannot sing,
Some other frolic he must bring,
To make the festive chamber ring,
For now's the time of Christmas.

If he says he can't do so,
That man is the season's foe.
Into the stocks that man must go,
For now's the time of Christmas!

Ringler MS Index 884. Balliol College, Oxford, MS 354. Fifteenth century. Unique.

61

Caput apri refero,   *"I bring the boar's head,*
Resonens laudes Domino.   *Sounding praises to the Lord." (burden)*

The boar's head in my hands I bring
With garlands gay and birds to sing.
Now help me make the chamber ring,
    Qui estis in convivio.   *"All those gathered here"*

The boar's head, I understand,
Is the finest service in the land,
Wherever it may come to hand,
    Servitur cum sinapio.   *"Served up with mustard"*

The boar's head, yet I say,
Lingers till the twelfth-most day,
Then takes its leave and goes away,
    Exivit tunc de patria.   *"It has left the country."*

Ringler MS Index 1502. Balliol College, Oxford, MS 354. Fifteenth century. Unique.

62[17]

Deo gracias anglia,   *"Offer thanks to God, England, for victory." (burden)*
Redde pro victoria.

Our king went forth to Normandy
With grace and mighty chivalry.
There God upheld him wondrously
So England may proclaim with glee:
    Deo gracias!   *"Thanks be to God."*

He set a siege, as all men say,
To Harfleur town in royal array.
That town he wrung. He made it pay,

17. Commemorates Henry V's victory at Agincourt in 1415.

As France will ever rue, we pray.
   Deo gracias!

Then passed our king with all his host
Through France, for all the Frenchmen's boast.
He steered his course back toward the coast,
Marched on till Agincourt was close.
   Deo gracias!

And there in truth the comely knight
Engaged the French and led the fight.
Through God's great grace and holy might
He won the field before that night.
   Deo gracias!

French earls and dukes and other lords
Were swiftly slain without their swords.
To London others came as wards,
As that great, joyful tale records.
   Deo gracias!

May gracious God now save our king,
His people too, we pray, and bring
Him happy life, death with no sting,
So we at length may safely sing:
   Deo gracias!

Index 2716. Bodleian MS 3340. Musical setting. Fifteenth century. Not unique.

63

Ah, dear God, how can it be,
   That all things wear and waste away?
Friendship is but vanity.
   It seldom lasts a single day.
   Friends are rarely what they say.
      They're quick to take; to give, they're not.

In good times they accept their pay,
　　But seldom seen is soon forgot.

I speak in earnest, lords, not play,
　　And thus I pray you to take heed: 10
If you consider what I say,
　　You'll see the truth of it indeed.
　　For simple shame your hearts will bleed.
　　　His strength availed him not a jot.
　　For he who made our nation speed
　　　Is seldom seen and soon forgot.

Once we had an English ship—
　　A noble ship, tall as a tower.
Through Christendom it bore the whip,
　　Our bulwark in the darkest hour.   20
　　It weathered well the sharpest shower
　　　And each extreme of cold or hot.
　　But now this ship, of ships the flower,
　　　Is seldom seen and soon forgot.

The ship depended on a rudder
　　That steered its course and governed it.
In all the world there's not another
　　Of equal virtue, I submit.
　　While ship and rudder still were knit,
　　　They feared no storm or fight or plot.   30
　　But now they're rent apart, lords, split,
　　　And seldom seen is soon forgot.

Through any waves that ship once sailed.
　　In every sea it rode secure.
In every weather it prevailed,
　　While its rudder yet endured.
　　Though seas were raging or demure,
　　　That ship would make its sheltered spot.
　　But now the ship, you may be sure,
　　　Is seldom seen and soon forgot.   40

To this ship may be compared
   The arms and strength of our fair land.
These once seemed weak as men declared
   All over France, I understand.
     But when the Frenchmen felt our hand,
       Their nation soon bewailed its lot.
     King John[18] himself came here in bands,
       But now all this has been forgot.

That ship had a steadfast mast.
   Its rugged sails were trim and sealed.   50
The ship was fearless to the last—
   Strong to fight and never yield.
     It launched a barge upon the field
       That feared the Frenchmen not a jot.
     That barge, good sirs, was England's shield,
       But now it's gone and long forgot.

The rudder was not oak or elm,
   But Edward the Third, the noble knight.[19]
The prince, his son,[20] held up his helm
   And seldom gave an inch in fight.   60
     The king put forth his power aright;
       The prince feared neither blade nor shot.
     But now we weigh them both full light,
       For seldom seen is soon forgot.

The fighting barge was our Duke Henry,[21]
   A noble knight and one well tried.
He served his lord upon the sea,
   Accepting battles in his stride.

---

18. John II (1319–64). He was captured in the Hundred Years' War in 1359 and died in England.

19. Reigned 1327–77.

20. Edward the Black Prince (1330–76). He defeated the French at Poitiers in 1556 and successfully invested Paris in 1560.

21. Henry of Grosmont (1300–61), first Duke of Lancaster.

When men opposed him in their pride,
    He gave them better than he got.   70
But now that noble duke has died,
    And seldom seen is soon forgot.

The English Commons, by the Cross,
    I liken to the ship's strong mast.
Who with their goods, at heavy cost,
    Maintained the war from first to last.
    The wind that moved us by its blast—
        The nation's prayers—preserved our lot.
But now devotion's overpassed,
    And all those deeds are clean forgot.   80

Yet, though these lords are laid full low,
    Their stock springs from the selfsame root.
And now a sapling starts to grow;[22]
    I pray we'll profit by this shoot.
    May he grind foemen underfoot,
        And may a long reign be his lot.
Jesus grant him high repute,
    So seldom seen is not forgot!

And when that shoot is fully grown,
    Nursed by kindly soil and shower,   90
I hope he shall be widely known
    Among the nations for his power.
    May his life and limbs both flower;
        May he bear arms just as he ought.
Jesus grant the boy his hour,
    So seldom seen is not forgot!

And so I say now, use your might
    To help this young sprig wax and grow.
Let every man maintain his right,

22. Richard II (1367–99), son of the Black Prince. He was ten years old when he came to the throne in 1377.

Upholding him—both high and low.   100
Then let the Frenchmen boast and blow
   Their empty threats, the idle sots.
We must be wicked men and slow
   If seldom seen is soon forgot.

Remember how, and not long since,
   Your doughty king died in his age.
Recall his Edward, our great prince,
   A man of martial might, yet sage.
   None finer ever trod our stage,
      Nor can their strength and might be taught.   110
   Weigh this well, our loss to gauge,
      So seldom seen is not forgot.

Index 5. Bodleian MS 3938. Fifteenth century. Not unique.

64

Lyard is an old horse and can no longer draw.
He shall be put to pasture. On holly he must chaw.
There he shall go limping, alone, without a shoe,
For he is but an old horse with nothing else to do.
As long as he could pull his weight, so long was Lyard loved.
They brought him his provender, and let him eat thereof.
But now he cannot do the deeds that he could do before,
They feed him only bean stalks. Good grain he sees no more.
They lead him to the smithy, to take his shoes away,
And turn him out into the woods to forage as he may.
Whoever can no longer work must go the same way too—
Wander barefoot in the woods. That's all that he is due.

Index 2026. Lincoln Cathedral MS 91. Fifteenth century. Unique.

65

Some men say my looks are dark,
But, sirs, I don't regret my hue.

My love flies strongly to its mark,
Although I'm not as white as you.

Black is a color and it's good,
So say I and many more.
My hat is black; so is my hood,
And all the ones I've worn before.

Black will do as good a deed
As any white at board or bed,
And black is true in any need
As white can be, upon my head.

Wind and water stain the white,
And yet the black they cannot stain.
Where black is seen, there's my delight.
Lo, reason makes black's virtues plain.

Pepper's black at any price,
But crack it and it is not so.
Let go the color; take the spice.
The black serves well; that much I know.

God save all them whose looks are brown;
They're true as steel, as I can tell.
God keep them both in field and town.
If so, I shall be kept full well.

Index 3174. Gonville and Caius College, Cambridge, MS 383. Fifteenth century. Unique.

66

At the north end of silver white
    My love bid me—
At the north end of silver white
My love bid me I should abide.
I laid my goods, broad as a shield,
    And, Lord, he smote—

I laid my goods, broad as a shield,
   And, Lord, he smote thereon.
No man shall ever joust thereat,
   Unless he can—
No man shall ever joust thereat,
   Unless he can hit home.

At the south end of silver white
   My love bid me—
At the south end of silver white
My love bid me I should abide.
I laid my goods, a peck's worth wide,
   And, Lord, he smote—
I laid my goods, a peck's worth wide,
   And, Lord, he smote thereon.
No man shall ever joust thereat,
   Unless he can—
No man shall ever joust thereat,
   Unless he can hit home.

At the west end of silver white
   My love bid me—
At the west end of silver white
My love bid me I should abide.
I laid my goods, a bushel broad,
   And, Lord, he smote—
I laid my goods, a bushel broad,
   And, Lord, he smote thereon.
No man shall ever joust thereat,
   Unless he can—
No man shall ever joust thereat,
   Unless he can hit home.

Index 438. Cambridge University Additional MSS 5943. Fifteenth century. Unique.

67

I have twelve oxen, fair and brown.
They go to graze below the town.

  With hay! With how! With hay!
Did you see my oxen, you pretty little boy?

I have twelve oxen, fair and white.
They go to graze upon the height.
    With hay! With how! With hay!
Did you see my oxen, you pretty little boy?

I have twelve oxen, fair and black.
They go to graze beside the track.
    With hay! With how! With hay!
Did you see my oxen, you pretty little boy?

I have twelve oxen, fair and red.
They go to graze where they are led.
    With hay! With how! With hay!
Did you see my oxen, you pretty little boy?

Ringler MS Index 649. Balliol College, Oxford, MS 354. Sixteenth century. Unique.

68[23]

The foremost of these beastly three
Is worst of all, it seems to me:

The Lion

The lion, sirs, is wondrous strong,
And guileful in each way.
And whether he play
Or take his prey,
He cannot help but slay.

23. The beasts here may refer to specific political figures of the time.

The Bear

Beware the bear, sirs, have a care,
For look, the bear will bite.
He's seldom met, as I declare,
But he will bite or smite.

The Dragon

"I can swallow all that I've caught.
But some I will save, and some I will not."

Index 3353. British Library, MS Harley 7322. Fourteenth century. Unique.

69

Black, swarthy smiths smattered with smoke
Drive me toward death with the din of their dints!
Such noise in the night no man has heard ever.
What knavish calls! What a clatter of knocks!
The crooked curs cry, "Coal here! More coal!"
And blow on their bellows till their brains are bursting.
"Huff, puff," says one. "Haff, paff," says the other.
They spit and sprawl and sputter by spells.
They gnaw and gnash and groan together,
And keep themselves hot by smiting their hammers.
Their long leather aprons are of tough bull's hide
To shield their shanks from the singeing sparks.
Heavy hammers they have, and smash them down hard—
Stark strokes ringing on shrieking steel.
"Luss, buss! Lass, dass!" they sound out by turns.
Accursed is their clamor. The Devil dispel it!
The master lengthens a little piece, draws out a lesser one,
Twines them together, his blows ringing treble:
"Tick, tack, hick, hack, ticket, tacket, tick, tack."
"Luss, buss! Lass, dass!" What a life these churls lead!
Armorers, steel smiths, Christ bring them sorrow!
Their strokes and steel-hissing shatter our sleep!

Index 3227. British Library, MS Arundel 292. Thirteenth century. Unique.

70

I have a young sister,
Far beyond the sea.
Many are the dainty things
My sister sent to me.

She sent me a cherry
Without a stone.
She sent me a dove
Without a bone.

She sent me a briar bush
Without a branch to burn.
She bid me love my sweetheart
But nevermore to yearn.

How could there be a cherry
Without a stone?
How could there be a dove
Without a bone?

How could there be a briar
Without a branch to burn?
How could I love my sweetheart
Yet never yearn?

When the cherry was a flower,
It had no stone.
When the dove was in its egg,
It had no bone.

When the briar was a seed,
It had no branch to burn.
When a maiden has her sweetheart,
She has no call to yearn.

Index 1303. British Library, MS Sloane 2593. Fifteenth century. Unique.

71[24]

The maiden in the moor lay,
    In the moor lay,
Seven nights full, seven nights full.
The maiden in the moor lay,
    In the moor lay,
Seven nights full and a day.

Good was what she ate.
And what did she eat?
    The primrose and the . . .
    The primrose and the . . .
Good was what she ate.
And what did she eat?
    The primrose and the violet.

Good was what she drank.
And what did she drink?
    Cold water from the . . .
    Cold water from the . . .
Good was what she drank.
And what did she drink?
    Cold water from the spring.

Good was her bower.
And what was her bower?
    The red rose and the . . .
    The red rose and the . . .
Good was her bower.
And what was her bower?
    The red rose and the lily flower.

Index 2037.5. Bodleian, MS Rawlinson D. 913. Fourteenth century. Not unique.

24. This strange poem has sometimes been thought to concern the Virgin Mary, but it was
condemned by a fourteenth-century bishop who supplied a set of Latin lyrics to be sung to the
same melody. Other explanations involve witchcraft, Celtic mythology, and folk rituals.

72

I've been a forester many a day;
I'm now grown gray and poor.
I'll hang my horn on the greenwood spray,
A forester no more.

And yet while I can bend my bow,
I shall not wed a wife.
I'll build a bower in woods I know,
And there I'll lead my life.

Ringler MS Index 643. British Library, Additional MSS 5665. Musical setting. Sixteenth century. Unique.

Snatches

Inhalt

Snatches

The poems in this section include memory joggers like "Thirty days . . ." (73), proverbs such as "When Adam dug . . ." (93), and a number of pieces that defy classification. Some are charming style exercises, like the calendar poem (74), which can hardly have been meant as a serious teaching device. Others are evocative fragments like "Merry sang the monks at Ely" (86), probably the oldest piece in the book, or the haunting "I am of Ireland" (83), which captivated William Butler Yeats, providing a title and refrain to one of his better-known poems.

While the mnemonic tags and proverbs here seem complete as they stand, other scraps could be bits of almost anything. On occasion it isn't even apparent where they should begin and end. For instance, the seemingly joyous snippet "Door, open softly" (105) appears on the same manuscript page as another pair of disconnected lines: "Ne saltou never, levedi,/ Tuynklen wyt thin eyen."[1] By itself, "Door, open softly" seems to celebrate a successful love encounter; but if the "Ne saltou" lines were meant to go with it, the speaker's having done his "will" could have a much more ominous meaning.

In general, though, these short pieces provide a glimpse of a largely commonsensical culture with a sturdy, even smug, reliance on everyday experience, the world of John the Carpenter in Chaucer's "Miller's Tale." Weeds are uprooted, cats quarrel, wise men fail, men drink beer or play football, and "Walter Pollard is a dullard" (99).

The Poems

73

Thirty days has November,
April, June, and September;

---

1. "Now shall you never, lady, / Twinkle with your eyes." See Bennett, p. 365.

Of twenty-eight is but one,
And all the rest have thirty-one.

Index 3571. British Library, MS Harley 2341. Fifteenth century. Not unique.

74

January	By the fire I warm my hands.
February	I take my spade and dig my lands.
March	Here I set my seeds to spring.
April	Now I hear the small birds sing.
May	I am as light as a bird in a tree.
June	I uproot any weed I see.
July	I scythe the meadow, making hay.
August	I cut my grain the selfsame way.
September	With my flail I earn my bread.
October	I take my winter wheat to spread.
November	At Martinmas I kill my swine. *November 11*
December	At Christmastide I drink red wine.

Index 579. Bodleian MS 1689. Fifteenth century. Not unique.

75

If Paul's feast day be fair and clear,   *January 25*
Why then, expect a happy year.
But if it chance to snow or rain,
Up will go the price of grain.
And if the wind blows high and far,
The kingdom will be roiled by war.
If storm clouds blacken all the sky,
Your cattle and your fowl will die.

Index 1423. Dunrobin Castle, Scotland. Fifteenth century. Unique.

76

Thirty-two teeth that are full keen,
Two hundred bones and then nineteen,

Three hundred veins plus sixty-five,
Has every mortal man alive.

Index 3572. Bodleian MS 14526. Fifteenth century. Unique.

77

Phlegmatic	Sluggy, slow, spitting much, Cold and moist, sirs, I am such. Dull and fat, pale and strange, That's what I am; I cannot change.
Sanguine	Liberal, I, loving and glad, Laughing, playing, seldom sad; Rosy, singing, bold to fight, Hot and moist, quick to ignite.
Choleric	I'm sad and heavy in my thought. I covet much, surrender naught. Tricky, subtle, cold, and dry: A yellow-colored mope am I.
Melancholy	Envious, crooked, rough-skinned, strong, I spend too much and live too long. Scheming, skinny, dry, and hot, I'm never pleased with what I've got.

Index 3157. Lambeth Palace MS 523. Fifteenth century. Unique.

78

Fresh goat's gall with juice of leeks
Helps deaf men hear when someone speaks.
Two parts of juice, a third of gall—
Mixed up well and warmed withal—
Shot up the nose or in the ear,
Will make the sharpest headache clear.
The same will knit a broken bone,
Or drain a sore that's pussy grown.

Leek juice and salt, two to one,
Will ease a woman's menstrual run.
A drunken man who wakes in pain
May eat a leek to cool his brain.

Index 1810. Huntington Library MS HU 1051. Fifteenth century. Unique.

79

Spend and God shall send.
Spare and shake with care.
No penny, no ware,
No goods and no care.
   Go, penny, go!

Index 3209. Gonville and Caius College, Cambridge, MS 261. Fourteenth century. Not unique.

80

I had my			and my		
I lent my	} goods		to my	} friend	
I asked my			of my		
I lost my			and my		

I turned my friend into my foe.
God grant that I no more do so.

Index 1297. British Library, MS Harley 116. Fifteenth century. Not unique.

81

Peace makes plenty.
Plenty makes pride.
Pride breeds dispute.
Poverty's the fruit.
Poverty makes peace.

Index 2742. Cambridge University Folio MS 1.6. Fifteenth century. Not unique.

82

Keep well the ten and shun the seven.
Rule well your five, and come to heaven.

Index 1817. Bodleian MS 14526. Fifteenth century. Not unique.

83

I am of Ireland.
I'm from the holy land
Of Ireland.

And so, good sir, I pray thee,
In hope of blessed charity
That you will come and dance with me
In Ireland.

Index 1008. Bodleian, MS Rawlinson D. 913. Fourteenth century. Unique.

84

Alanus calvus
Iacet hic sub marmore duro;
Utrum sit salvus
Non curavit, neque curo.

Anglice: *"in English"*

Here lies, beneath his marble stone,
Wealthy Alan, whose bald head shone.
Whether his soul was saved and why,
He never cared. No more do I.

Index 1207. British Library, MS Harley 665. Fifteenth century. Unique.

85

"All gold, Janet, is your hair.
All gold, Janet, is your hair."
"Just as yours is, John, my dear.
Just as yours is, John, my dear.
Like yours alone, my dear."

Index 179. Bodleian, MS Rawlinson D. 913. Fourteenth century. Unique.

86

Merry sang the monks at Ely
When Canute the king came rowing by.   *Danish king of England, c. 994–1035*
"Turn in," he said, "and row along,
So we may hear the monks in song."

Index 2164. Trinity College, Cambridge, MS 1105. Twelfth century. Not unique.

87

Make a wolf a priest, I say;
And send him to school, his psalms to say,
He'll back to the greenwood when he may.

Index 3513. British Library, Additional MSS 11579. Fourteenth century. Unique.

88

A man may beguile
His nature a while,
    With learning and lore.
And yet at the end
His nature won't bend,
    But be as before.

Ringler MS Index 25. British Library, MS Harley 116. Sixteenth century. Unique.

89

A bishop bookless,
A king guideless,
A young man reckless,
An old man witless,
A woman shameless—
I swear by heaven's king,
Those are five bitter things!

Index 1820. British Library, MS Harley 913. Fourteenth century. Not unique.

90

Watch well, Annot,
     Your chamber door.
It's you that Walter
     Is lusting for.

Index 3859.5. British Library, Cotton Faustina A. v. Fourteenth century. Unique.

91

Hope is hard when luck's its foe;
Luck will help the hopeless, though.
Lack-luck brings the world to woe.
May good luck with the righteous go!

Index 1251. British Library, MS Harley 2316. Fifteenth century. Unique.

92

The ax was sharp, the block was stained,
The fourth year that King Richard reigned.[2]   *Richard II*

Index 3306. St. John's College, Oxford, MS 209. Fifteenth century. Not unique.

93

When Adam dug and Eve spun,   *a populist rallying cry against hereditary nobles*
Who was then the gentle one?

Index 3922. Bodleian MS 15444. Fifteenth century. Not unique.

94

When the broom is in flower   *broom, a flowering shrub*
Young lads woo by the hour.

---

2. Richard's fourth year was 1381, the year of the Peasants' Revolt.

When the bloom's on the furse,   *gorse, another shrub*
Why, they woo even worse!

Index 3927.6. Trinity College, Cambridge, MS O.2.45. Thirteenth century. Unique.

95

Be it better, be it worse,
Follow him who holds the purse.

Index 465.5. Bodleian MS 1544. Fifteenth century. Not unique.

96

The smaller the peas, the more in the pot.
The fairer the woman, the looser she'll trot.

Index 3464.5. John Rylands Library Latin MS 394. Fifteenth century. Not unique.

97

Two women in one house,
Two cats with one mouse,
Two dogs with one bone,
Will not agree upon their own.

Ringler MS Index 1779. British Library, MS Lansdowne 762. Sixteenth century. Not unique.

98

There's not so wise a man
That he has mastered all.
There's not so strong a man
But he may take a fall.
There's not so false a man
That someone won't believe him.
There's not so meek a man
That someone cannot peeve him.

Index 3538. British Library, MS Harley 2251. Fifteenth century. Not unique.

99[3]

Walter Pollard is a dullard.
Walter, I say, is never gay.

Recorded in Sisam. Bodleian, MS Rawlinson D. 328. Fifteenth century. Unique.

100

This book is one;
God's curse another.
Who takes the one,
God send the other!

Index 3580. British Library, MS Harley 1251. Fifteenth century. Not unique.

101

Here I was and here I drank.
Farewell, dame, and take my thanks.
Here I sat and had good cheer.
Here I took my fill of beer.

Index 1201. Trinity College, Dublin, MS 214. Fifteenth century. Unique.

102

An old wife and an empty cup;
   No mirth in one or in the other.
A wedded man is well tied up;
   He may not choose another.

A young wife and an angry duck;
   Who can quack the best?
With either one a man is stuck;
   He'll have but little rest.

Index 3533.5. Bodleian MS 21831. Fifteenth century. Not unique.

   3. The subject, Walter Pollard of Plymouth, once owned the manuscript where this appears.

103

Bruised brawn and broken bones,
Strife and discord, beggared homes,
A crippled age (and lame before),
These football brings, and nothing more.

Recorded in Sisam. Magdalene College, Cambridge, Maitland Folio MS, p. 242. Sixteenth
century. Unique.

104

A garden walk and light for flowers,   *alley, sun = Alison*
That's my true love. Now who is yours?

Frozen water and Cain's good brother,   *ice, Abel = Isabel*
She is my lady and no other.

Index 597.5. Bodleian MS 2059. Fifteenth century. Not unique.

105

Door, open softly.
Open still and still.
This night I have within her bower
Done all my will, my will.

Index 2288. Worcester Cathedral Library MS Q.50. Fourteenth century. Unique.

106[4]

Alas, how may I sing?
What joy can my life bring?
I'm wed to that old man.

---

4. This fragment appears in *The Red Book of Ossory* to identify a song to which the bishop
there had written a new religious Latin text.

The one I love is banned,
The sweetest of all things.

Index 1265. Kilkenny, *The Red Book of Ossory.* Fourteenth century. Unique.

107

A merry time I tell in May
  When bright blossoms burst from the tree,
And birds sit singing night and day,
  And meadows laugh for glee.

Index 2162. Pembroke College, Cambridge, MS 258. Fourteenth century. Unique.

108[5]

"Tell me, man in the broom,   *thorny shrub*
What would you do in my room?
How can I make my husband be
In love with me?"

"Hold your tongue still.
You'll have your will."

Index 3078. Trinity College, Cambridge, MS 323. Thirteenth century. Not unique.

109

"Tell me, man in the broom,
What would you do in my room?
My husband is a wretched man;
You'll find no worse one in the land."

5. The man or "wight" in the broom, referred to in 108 and 109, may be some sort of wood spirit.

"If your husband is poor,
Keep still and endure."

Recorded in Penguin. British Library Additional MSS 11579. Thirteenth century. Unique.

110

Watch before you wed. Know before you're knotted.
Watch ere you wed, and then you can wait.
But knot ere you know and you'll rue it too late.
Consider the knot; don't hasten to try it.
"*Had I known what I know!*" comes too late to untie it.

Index 1829. Bodleian MS 1797. Fourteenth century. Not unique.

Religious Lyrics

Religious Lyrics

Not only does more religious than secular poetry survive from the Middle English period, but it survives in more places. Many of the lyrics in this section appear in several manuscripts, enough to suggest they were widely distributed and consulted as aids to piety. Some were set to music, often sharing their tunes with popular secular lyrics. At least two, "There is no rose . . ." (127) and the "Corpus Christi Carol" (157), are still sung today. Others may have been recited from the pulpit. One rich source of religious poetry is *The Commonplace Book of John Grimestone,* compiled by a fourteenth-century friar of Norfolk. Poems 113, 114, 115, 123, 124, 130, and 143 come from his collection of preaching materials preserved in the National Library of Scotland.

For all its abundance, though, Middle English religious poetry is somewhat predictable. Aside from buoyant reflections on the book of Genesis like "Adam lay bound" (111) and "In the vale of Abraham" (138), Middle English religious lyrics tend to focus raptly on the stories of Jesus and His mother Mary. None of these poems is at all subtle or complex: they return again and again to the outward details of Christ's Passion and Nativity and Mary's compliancy and grief in an effort to make the reader or hearer sympathize with that holy pair, who are treated as almost equally sacred.

This approach resembles the Jesus-centered spirituality of the fourteenth-century English mystics Richard Rolle and Julian of Norwich, who above all strove to *see* and *feel* Mary's sorrows and Christ's crucifixion. Seeing and feeling are central to many Middle English poems about Christ's wounds, His humble birth, and Mary beside the Cross:

> White was His naked breast,
>   Bloody red His side,
> Wan was His lovely face,
>   His wounds were deep and wide.
>
> His straining arms were stretched out straight,
>   High upon the Cross.

> From five parts of His body
>> Streamed the blood He lost.   (122)

Word-pictures like this were intended to reach a broad audience. They marshal distinct appeals to the senses—white and red to be seen, deep wounds and straining sinews to be felt, and streaming blood almost to be tasted from where the speaker and we watch, low beneath the Cross.

At other times, Christ Himself speaks from the Cross or His mother's lap, usually to complain that His sacrifice has not been well enough appreciated by those He died to save. In one mini-epic, however, He equals any of the powerful heroes of Old English poetry:

> I labored sore and suffered death,
> And now I rest to draw my breath,
> But I shall come right soon in might.
> On heaven and earth my doom shall light,
> And then shall Satan know, and man,
> What I was and what I am.   (112)

Middle English religious poetry rarely sounds such resounding notes. More common is a sweet and simple sense of wonder, as in the famous lyric "I sing of a maiden matchless" (125), where the mystery of the Immaculate Conception is captured in a perfect series of homely but luminous similes.

The same concreteness and emotional clarity distinguish Middle English poems on death, another engrossing topic. These pieces relentlessly focus on humankind's unworthiness, the transience of pleasure, and the sights and smells of the grave, providing a useful counterweight to the worldliness of the secular lyrics. What is the world? Nothing but dirt. And so are we, as this disdainful riddle makes unforgettably plain:

> Earth took earth from earth with woe.
> Earth drew earth to the earth below.
> Earth laid out earth in earthen stuff.
> And then had earth of earth enough.   (144)

The Poems

111

Adam lay bound,
Bound up in a bond.
Four thousand winters
He thought not too long.   *ironic*
And all was for an apple,
An apple that he took,
As learned men find written,
Written in their book.

Had not the apple taken been,
The apple taken been,
Then had not our lady
Become our heaven's queen.
Blessed be the time
That apple taken was.
And therefore we must sing:
"Deo gracias!"   *"Thanks be to God!"*

Index 117. British Library, MS Sloane 2593. Fifteenth century. Unique.

112

I labored sore and suffered death,
And now I rest to draw my breath,
But I shall come right soon in might.
On heaven and earth my doom shall light,
And then shall Satan know, and man,
What I was and what I am.

Index 1308. National Library of Scotland, Advocates 19.1.11. Fifteenth century. Unique.

113[1]

Love me brought,
And love me wrought,
Man, to be thy friend.

Love me fed,
And love me led
And left me to my end.

Love me slew,
And love me drew
And laid me on my bier.

Love only knows,
For love I chose
Mankind to buy most dear.

So now dread naught;
I have thee sought,
Pursuing day and night.

I'll shelter thee.
I paid the fee.
I won thee in my fight.

Index 2012. National Library of Scotland, Advocates 18.7.21. Fourteenth century. Unique.

114

I am Jesus, come to fight
Without a shield or spear.
Consider, man—you'd die aright,
Had I not suffered here.

1. This and the following two poems come from *The Commonplace Book of John Grimestone.*

But since I came to you and brought
Sweet aid for each and all,
Unlock your heart, tell me your thought,
Your sins both great and small.

Index 1274. National Library of Scotland, Advocates 18.7.21. Fourteenth century. Unique.

115

Sinful man, when will you see
The pain I bore for love of thee?
I call out though my life has fled.
My hands and feet were pierced and spread.
I was nailed upon the tree;
Died and was buried, man, for thee.
All this I suffered for your sake,
And yet I feel a sharper ache,
When you pull back or turn away,
Than all my torments on that day.

Index 3109. National Library of Scotland, Advocates 18.7.21. Fourteenth century. Not unique.

116

Good Saint Steven was a clerk
    Within King Herod's hall
And served him bread upon a cloth
    As such things oft befall.

Steven from the kitchen came,
    A boar's head in his hand.
He saw a star shine fair and bright
    Where Bethlehem must stand.

At that he cast the boar's head down
    And went into the hall.   10
"I forsake you, king," he said,
    "You and your works all!

"I forsake you, Herod, king,
    Whatever shall befall.
A child was born this very night
    Far better than us all."

"What ails you, Steven?" said the king.
    "What holds you in thrall?
Lack you either meat or drink
    Here within my hall?"   20

"I lack neither meat or drink,
    King, within your hall,
But one was born this very night
    Far better than us all."

"What ails you, Steven? Are you mad?
    Or do you start to rave?
Lack you either gold or fees
    Or aught that you would have?"

"I lack neither gold or fees
    Or aught else I would have.   30
A child was born in Bethlehem;
    He's come the world to save."

"If so," proclaimed the wicked king,
    "Then this is true as well.
This capon[2] lying in my dish
    Shall sing out like a bell!"

The king's last word was hardly out,
    His speech within the hall,
When the bird crowed *Christus natus est*   *Christ is born.*
    Among the high lords all.   40

---

2. A capon is a rooster that has been neutered. Since this one has been killed and cooked as well, its crowing appears doubly unlikely.

The king called his tormenters,
  By one and two and three.
"Take this Steven out," he said,
  "And stone him by a tree."

They led forth good Saint Steven
  And stoned him in the way,
And therefore is his even
  The night of Christmas Day.[3]

Index 3058. British Library, MS Sloane 2593. Fifteenth century. Unique.

117[4]

O man unkind,
Keep thou in mind
My dying hurt.
Thou shall me find
A friend full kind:
Lo, here, my heart.

Index 2507. Trinity College, Cambridge, MS 1157. Fifteenth century. Not unique.

118

Jesus Christ, my lover sweet,
That died to save me on the tree,
With all my heart I now beseech,
By those five wounds that injured thee,
That just as fast within my heart
Your sacred love may rooted be
As was the spear that pierced your side
When you were struck and died for me.

Index 1684. British Library, MS Harley 2316. Fourteenth century. Not unique.

3. St. Steven's day is December 26, so its eve is on the twenty-fifth.
4. This poem is written out beside a drawing on the same page of Christ covered in wounds.

119

Sweet Jesus, king of happiness,
My heart's love, my heart's bliss,
Nothing's sweet as your caress.
Woe to him you do not bless!

Sweet Jesus, my heart's light,
You are full day without a night.
Give me, Lord, more strength and might
To answer your sweet love aright.

Sweet Jesus, my heart's fruit,
In my heart affix a root,
And let it flourish by my suit
Till it becomes a springing shoot.

Index 3236. Bodleian MS 1687. Thirteenth century. Not unique.

120[5]

My Lord, when you called out to me,
I answered nothing back to thee
But these words, slow and sleepy:
"Bide yet! Bide a little!"
The end of "yet" is far, however,
And "bide a little" goes on forever.

Index 1978. New College, Oxford, MS 88. Fourteenth century. Unique.

121

"Lullay, my child, and weep no more.
  Sleep, dear babe, be still.
The King of Bliss, your Father is.
  You've come here by His will."   (burden)

5. Based on a passage from St. Augustine's *Confessions,* Book VIII, Chapter V.

The other night
I saw a sight,
   A maid her cradle blessed.
She rocked and crooned.
This was her tune:
   "Lullay, my child, now rest."

"I cannot sleep,
But I must weep,
   I am so woebegone.
Sleep I would   10
But I am cold,
   And covering have I none."

The babe spoke thus.
His words were just,
   As to the maid he prayed:
"My mother dear,
Why am I here
   And in this cradle laid?

"I was born
On Christmas morn   20
   Beside the ox and ass.
My mother mild,
I am your child,
   But He my Father was.

"Adam's guilt
All mankind spilt.
   That sin grieved me full sore.
O man, for thee
Here I shall be
   For thirty winters more.   30

"I'll be assailed,
Mocked, scourged, and nailed,
   To die atop a hill.

My death and I
Mankind will buy.
  It is my Father's will.

"A spear so smart
Shall pierce my heart
  For all that I have done.
Say, Father, why   40
Have you on high
  Forgot your little son?"

Index 3596. Bodleian MS 29734. Fourteenth century. Not unique.

122

White was His naked breast,
  Bloody red His side,
Wan was His lovely face,
  His wounds were deep and wide.

His straining arms were stretched out straight,
  High upon the Cross.
From five parts of His body
  Streamed the blood He lost.

Index 4088. Durham Cathedral MS A.III.12. Thirteenth century. Not unique.

123[6]

Lovely tear of lovely eye,
Why do you bring me woe?
Sorrowful tear of sorrowful eye,
You burst my heart in two.   *(burden)*

You sigh full sore;
Your sorrow's more
  Than any tongue can tell.

6. This and the following poem come from *The Commonplace Book of John Grimestone.*

You sigh and sing;
Mankind you bring
  Out from the pit of hell.

I'm proud and keen;
You're meek and clean,
  Devoid of harm or guile.
You died for me;
I live through thee,
  Made blessed by your trial.

Your heart is rent;
Your body bent
  Upon the bloody tree.
Clouds part at last,
The fiend surpassed,
  Dear Christ, and all through thee!

Index 3691. National Library of Scotland, Advocates 18.7.21. Fourteenth century. Unique.

124

Lullay, lullay, little child. Child, now rest a throw.
From blessed heaven you came down to live here low.
Poor and little you were made and sent unknown,
To suffer pain for all our sins, but not your own.
  Lullay, lullay, little child, your grief's well taken.
  You were sent into this world as if forsaken.

Lullay, lullay, little lad, king over all.
When I consider your great harm, my spirits fall.
What can I feel but sorrow if love is in my heart?
I know the pains you'll suffer, none else so smart.   10
  Lullay, lullay, little child, well may you cry.
  Your body will lie white and cold before you die.

Child, this is a vale of tears, a place of danger.
Your ragged clothes prove this full well, your lowly manger.

Cold and hunger you'll endure, though free of sin,
And then you'll die upon the Cross for love of men.
   Lullay, lullay, little child, in all your pain,
     You've come among your mortal foes. They'll be your bane.

Lullay, lullay, little child, your tears should flood
For anguish that will wring from you a sweat of blood.   20
Naked, bound up, you shall be. Sharp blows will rain.
Not one inch of precious flesh go free of pain.
   Lullay, lullay, little child, regard your weakness—
     The love of man that holds you bound, your mortal meekness.

Lullay, lullay, little child. Dear child, your grace!
All the suffering you bear, you bear in mankind's place.
If we were kind and good enough, lived by your lore,
The trials that you fear ahead would be no more.
   Lullay, lullay, little child, sleep soft and fast.
     In sorrow ends each earthly love but yours at last.   30

Index 2023. National Library of Scotland, Advocates 18.7.21. Fourteenth century. Unique.

125

I sing of a maiden matchless.[7]
The King of Kings
She bore in bliss.

He came as still
Where His mother was
As dew in April
Falling on the grass.

He came as still
To His mother's bower
As dew in April
Falling on the flower.

   7. *Makeles,* the word the author used here, can also mean "mateless" or "immaculate" in Middle English.

He came as still
Where His mother lay
As dew in April
Falling on the spray.

Mother and yet maiden
No woman was but she.
Well may such a lady
God's dear mother be.

Index 1367. British Library, MS Sloane 2593. Fifteenth century. Unique.

126

Now goes the sun beneath the wood.
I pity, Mary, your fair rood.[8]
Now goes the sun beneath the tree.
I pity, Mary, thy son and thee.

Index 2320. Bodleian MS 3462. Thirteenth century. Not unique.

127

There is no rose of such virtue
As is the rose that bore Jesu.
  Alleluia!

For in this rose, this blessed place,
Was heaven in a little space.
  Res miranda.   "a miracle"

By that rose all men can see
That He is God in persons three.
  Pari forma.   "in the same way"

---

  8. *Rood* is a pun. The word can refer to Mary's face, but also to the Cross.

The angels sang to shepherds so:
"Gloria in excelsis Deo."   "glory to God in the highest"
    Gaudeamus!   "Rejoice!"

Then let us leave all worldly mirth
And now attend His joyful birth.
    Transeamus.   "Let us cross over."

Index 3536. Trinity College, Cambridge, MS O.3.58. Musical setting. Fifteenth century.
    Not unique.

128

Of one that is so fair and bright,
    Velud maris stella,   "like a star at sea"
Brighter than the day's full light,
    Parens et puella,   "maiden mother"
Oh, hear my plea. Dear mother, see.
Lady, pray thy son for me,
    Tam pia,   "so devout"
That I at last may come to thee,
    Maria.

Lady, flower of everything,   10
    Rosa sine spina,   "rose without a thorn"
You bore our Jesus, heaven's king,
    Gratia divina.   "by divine grace"
Over all you bear the prize,
Lady, queen of Paradise,
    Electa,   "chosen"
Mother mild and maid as well,
    Effecta.   "perfected"

To counsel sorrow you are best,
    Felix fecundata.   "happy mother"
    To the weary, you are rest,
    Mater honorata.   "honored mother"

Beseech your Son, who with His blood
Released on us a healing flood
   In cruce,   *"on the Cross"*
That we all may come to Him
   In luce.   *"illuminated"*

All the world became forlorn
   Eva peccatrice,   *"through sinful Eve"*
Until Christ Our Lord was born   30
   De te, genitrice.   *"from you, our mother"*
The angel drove all sins away.
Farewell night, and welcome day
   Salutis.   *"of well-being"*
The well of grace sprang out of thee
   Virtutis.   *"of virtue"*

Well He knows He is your son,
   Ventre quem portasti.   *"whom you carried in the womb"*
He will not deny you soon,
   Parvum quem lactasti.   *"the little boy you suckled"*
So loving and so good He is,
He has brought us into bliss
   Superni.   *"supernal"*
He has shut the loathsome pit
   Inferni.   *"infernal"*

Index 2645. British Library, MS Egerton 613. Thirteenth century. Not unique.

129

Upon a lady my love is placed;
I won't seek someone new.
She's lovely, mild, much to my taste;
Her like I never knew.

This lady's fixed within my heart;
My love for her is sound.

I love her strongly, for my part;
My heart to her is bound.

I will not have another spouse
Nor other lovers take.
To her alone I take my vows;
All others I forsake.

This lady gentle is and meek,
Our mother and our health.
Nor is she ever far to seek,
Our helpmeet and our wealth.

At hand she is by night or day,
To woman, man, or child,
Who offer to her as they pray
A spirit undefiled.

To serve this lady we are bound,
In every time and place.
In yard or chamber, field or town,
We must implore her grace.

All pray, then, to this lady bright,
As to the blessed Trinity.
To bring our souls to heaven's light.
Amen, we say, for charity.

Index 3836. British Library, MS Cotton Caligula A. ii. Fifteenth century. Unique.

130[9]

As I lay out one night,
I looked upon a shore.
I saw a maiden bright;
A little child she bore.

9. From *The Commonplace Book of John Grimestone.*

The lady was so lovely,
Her manner was so kind,
My sharpest sorrows, surely,
Were banished from my mind.

I wondered at her beauty;
I marveled at her grace.   10
"Mankind is cheated, truly,"
I said, "if she's not chaste."

Beside her sat a sergeant,
A solemn man, I saw.
He seemed by his stern semblance
A man of God's Old Law.

His hair was thin and graying,
His color going pale.
He heard what I was saying
And stayed me with his tale.   20

"You wonder," he said, "doubtless,
On what you now see here.
I too, as I confess,
Till all became more clear:

"I say a woman can
Be maid and mother both—
Without the stain of man,
Give birth, upon my oath.

"Though I don't merit her,
She's Mary and my wife.   30
God knows she's clean and pure.
I love her as my life.

"Before I was aware
Her womb began to rise.

I tell you, and I swear,
I knew not in what wise.

"I trust in her true heart.
She never would do wrong.
She's blameless for her part,
And I have known her long.   40

"A thousand maidens should
Without a man conceive
Ere she would turn from good
And Joseph so deceive.

"The child that seems so poor—
In rags He lies content—
Was once and shall be more.
From God's house He was sent.

"His father's king of heaven
(And so said Gabriel).   50
That little child is even
Our Lord Emmanuel."

I heard and looked again.
It was as Joseph said:
The child was God and man;
His mother was a maid.

Each word of his I savored
With all my heart and might.
But then the vision wavered
And vanished from my sight.   60

This child now let us love
Each step along our way,
And see His face above
In heaven's perfect day.

Index 353. National Library of Scotland, Advocates 18.7.21. Musical setting. Fourteenth
    century. Not unique.

131

A shield of red, a cross of green,
A crown of thorns both long and keen,
A spear, a sponge, with nails three,
A body hanging on a tree—
Who to heart this shield will take
Among his foes need never quake.

Index 91. Bodleian MS 2156. Fourteenth century. Not unique.

132

God go with truth where it may be.
That's not in England, as we see.   *(burden)*

A man who goes the truth to tell
With great high lords he mustn't dwell,
For, sirs, as every clerk knows well,
    Truth suits men of low degree.

In ladies' chambers he'll be mute,
For there plain truth cannot set foot.
Though he would speak, it will not suit
    Among the best society.

Men of law give him no space.
Truth's no more mocked in any place.
I think they have but little grace
    To treat the truth so scornfully.

In holy church he mustn't sit.
From hand to hand they'd make him flit.
They value God's truth not a whit.
    Oh, truth, what shall become of thee?

Religious orders—solemn, sad—
If he go there, I hold him mad.

They'd strip him naked, and unclad
   They'd send him forth despitefully.

A true truth-seeker, not beguiled,
Must seek truth simply, like a child,
In Mary's heart, serene and mild,
   For that is where it is, pardee.   *"by God"*

Index 72. British Library, MS Sloane 2593. Fifteenth century. Unique.

133

Who knows now, of all us here,
Where he shall be another year?   *(burden)*

Another year it may betide
This group will scatter far and wide.
Not one of us may here abide—
   For Christ may send us such a year.

Another year it may befall
The lowest man within this hall
Will top the others, one and all—
   For Christ may send us such a year.

These lords who think themselves so great,
Who threaten poor men soon and late,
May fall themselves beneath their fate—
   For Christ may send us such a year.

Index 320. British Library Additional MS 40166 (C3). Fifteenth century. Unique.

134[10]

Go, little book of holy commendation;
   I pray to God your good intent shall speed
And show the truth to rightful contemplation:

---

10. This poem was found attached to a commentary on the Psalms.

The many ways by which a good life leads,
And must, to blessedness in every need.
    Show forth His grace, I say, a balm that lasts,
So virtue has its just reward, indeed,
    And vice is punished well when life has passed.

Your matter is the law of God's high will;
    Your manner is to show us how He meant
For us to follow Him with all our skill.
    His path is true. When every thought is bent
    To do His will, it stretches our intent.
        We learn new ways of virtue while we strive
    To lead our life in justice till it's spent,
        And follow where God leads while we're alive.

If proper judges give your teaching grace,
    If they approve and hold you fit to read,
Be not afraid in any other place.
    With their support and blessing you may speed
    To all the Inns of Court and sow your seed   *lawyers' societies and schools*
        Within the waiting soil of their breasts.
    Show how God's law—no other course—can lead
        To everlasting love and bliss and rest.

Index 929. National Library of Scotland, Advocates 18.8.5. Fourteenth century. Unique.

135[11]

Steadfast Cross, among all others
You are a tree of sovereign price.
Branch and flower, there's not another
Like you on earth, in any guise.
Sweet are the nails, and sweet the tree,
And sweeter the burden that hangs from thee!

Index 3212. Merton College, Oxford, MS 248. Fourteenth century. Unique.

11. Translation of a stanza from the sixth-century Latin hymn "Pange, Lingua, gloriosi."

136

Worldly bliss lasts but a throw;
It comes and flits away anon.
The longer I have found it so,
The less I mourn for what has gone.
The greatest joy's so mixed with care—
Sorrow's blight and evil fare—
It proves at last but poor and bare.
It passes quickly as it's won.
All our pleasures, here or there,
Just swell our grief when they're withdrawn.   10

Every bliss that comes in life,
You must know, will end in weeping.
House and home and child and wife
Are lent to you, not yours for keeping.
You shall lose all you have here—
Everything that you hold dear—
When you lie upon your bier,
Stripped naked for your final sleeping.
The only trappings you'll have there
Will be the deeds your soul is reaping.   20

All the things you think you own
Shall vanish then and come to naught.
The man who has no good deeds sown
Cannot expect to harvest aught.
Consider, man, while you have might,
How to set your misdeeds right,
And work for good by day and night.
Turn now, before your end is wrought.
You don't know when, but Christ, our light,
Will ask account for all you've got.   30

Man, why set your thought and heart
On worldly bliss that's so soon passed?
Why work so hard and suffer smarts

For ends so slight and unsteadfast?
It's licking honey from a thorn
To gather things this world has borne.
Their bitterness will make you mourn.
Better men would be aghast
To waste their gifts and finest parts,
And bankrupt fall to hell at last.   40

Consider why Our Lord first wrought
This world and you. Cast off your pride.
Think how His great suffering bought
You and all the world beside.
He gave Himself. He was the price
To buy your bliss if you are wise.
Oh, think on that and purge your eyes
Of sin and see what you denied.
While there's still time, do as you ought—
Or let the Devil be your guide!   50

Time serves. You're still beneath the sun;
So set your mirror up and see
What to do and what to shun—
What to grasp and what to flee.
Every day before your eyes
The world rocks on, the strong man dies.
That world is where your future lies.
You'll die yourself, by God's decree.
This fortune comes to everyone;
Man wends toward death. He can't go free.   60

Each good you do will be repaid.
Each wicked deed must then be bought.
When your final bed is laid,
You shall receive as you have wrought.
Bethink you well, I say. Take heed!
Cleanse yourself of each misdeed,
So Christ may help you in your need.
Christ loves you, man! Think how He fought

To win you heaven by His aid.
That bliss shall last, and wither not.   70

Index 4223. British Library, MS Arundel 248. Musical setting. Fourteenth century. Not unique.

137

Each day three worries come to me,
Each one sore in its degree:
One, that I must go away.
Two, who knows the time or day?
And yet the third's my greatest care—
I don't know whither I shall fare.

Index 695. Jesus College, Oxford, MS 29. Fourteenth century. Not unique.

138

Now bethink you, gentle ones,
How Adam dug and Eve spun.   *(burden)*

In the vale of Abraham
Christ Himself made Adam man
And Eve his wife to serve His plan,
    And thus this ordered world began.

"Come now, Adam, here you see
The bliss of Paradise so free;
Within it stands an apple tree—
    Leaves and fruit appear thereon.

"Adam, if you eat that fruit,
You lose these joys, beyond dispute,   10
And gain the pains of hell to boot."
    Thus God Himself informed the man.

God spoke to Adam and was gone,
And, lo, here came the fiend anon—

A traitor through and through, that one—
    He saw the tree and climbed thereon.

"What ails you, sir? You're mad, I swear!
The Lord's your foe in this affair.
He would not have you know or share
    The wisdom that He has at hand.   20

"Take the apple off the tree
And eat thereof as I bid thee.
All His wisdom thou shalt see.
    And from thee then shall God hide none."

When Adam bit into the fruit
He lost all joy, beyond dispute.
He had no words, but stricken mute
    He stood there naked as a stone.

Next came an angel with a blade
To drive him from that pleasant glade.   30
And then was Adam sore afraid.
    What kind of life had he begun?

Index 1568. British Library, MS Sloane 2593. Fifteenth century. Unique.

139

Here I am, but go I must.
In Jesus Christ I put my trust.
May no misfortune cause me care,
Neither here nor anywhere.
Father uphold me; Son uphold me.
Holy Ghost and Trinity,
Come between my foes and me.
Defend me now on every coast.
Father, Son, and Holy Ghost.   Amen

Index 1199. Bodleian MS 7798. Fifteenth century. Unique.

140

All you who pass this holy place—
   Spiritual, temporal, of each degree—   *in holy orders or secular life*
Remember for a little space,
   I was like you; you'll be like me.
Now say for me in charity,
      To Jesus and His mother Mary,
      A *Pater Noster* and an *Ave.*   *Latin prayers*

Ringler MS Index 125. Trinity College, Cambridge, MS 366. Fifteenth century. Unique.

141

Upon my right side, as I lay,
Blessed Mother, I thee pray,
For the tears with which you dressed
Jesus' feet and body blest,
Send me now the grace to rest.
Let none but good dreams be my guest.
Sound sleep till morning grant to me.
Our Lord's the fruit; you were the tree.
All praise the bloom that sprang from thee!
In nomine Patris et Filii et Spiritus Sancti.   *"in the name of the Father,*
                                            Son, and Holy Ghost"

                    Amen.

Index 3844. British Library, MS Harley 541. Fifteenth century. Unique.

142[12]

The red cross of a Christian's creed
   Came at the head of my first book.
The words beneath were "God me speed,"
   The earliest lesson that I took.

12. This poem appears in several manuscripts of a translation of Bartholomew de Glanville's *De proprietatibus rerum,* a natural history collection. The translation was made by an English writer, John of Trevisa (c. 1326–c. 1402). The phrase "God speed me" is often associated with children's books (Robbins, pp. 260–61).

Next I learned my *a* and *b*
   And other letters by their names,
But always it was "God speed me"
   That helped me most in school or games.

Wherever I played, in fields or meads,
   I came back to this simple gloss.
I prayed for help in all my deeds
   Of Him that died upon the Cross.

Now childish play in Jesus' name
   I shall let go and start instead
This longer, more demanding game.
   I turn away, upon my head,

From pleasant woods and meads and fields,
   The places where I played before,
And in His name who all grace wields
   I gird for this, my latest chore.

I pray that God will speed my wits—
   I'll take what help He's pleased to send—
I'll play my best if He permits
   And bring this to a goodly end.

Index 33. Cambridge University, MS Ii.5.41. Thirteenth century. Not unique.

143[13]

Gold and all the joys we win
Are nothing but Our Savior's Cross.
I would be clad in Christ's poor skin,
That ran so long with blood He lost,
And in His heart take up my inn;
There's food, indeed, that needs no sauce.

13. From *The Commonplace Book of John Grimestone.*

I'd care no more for kith and kin.
God is good. All else is dross.

Index 1002. National Library of Scotland. Advocates 18.7.21. Fourteenth century. Unique.

144

Earth took earth from earth with woe.
Earth drew earth to the earth below.
Earth laid out earth in earthen stuff.
And then had earth of earth enough.

Index 3939. British Library, MS Harley 2253. Fourteenth century. Not unique.

145

I wend toward death, a sturdy knight.
I won the flower in every fight.
But all my power could not quell death.
I wend toward that with every breath.

I wend toward death, a sovereign king.
What good is all the world may bring?
Death waits down every human way.
I wend now to be clothed in clay.

I wend toward death, a clerk of skill.
My words bent all men to my will.
But death soon brought me to my end.
Be warned by me! To death I wend.

Index 1387. British Library, MS Cotton Faustina B. vii, Part II. Fifteenth century. Not unique.

146

When the turf is your tower,
And your pit is your bower,
Your flesh and concerns
Shall be eaten by worms.

What good to you then
All the world sought by men?

Index 4044. Trinity College, Cambridge, MS 323. Thirteenth century. Unique.

147

By nature's laws I came with pain
Into this world with tears and cries.
Little since has been my gain,
Quick to fall but slow to rise.
I'll suffer more when I am slain,
And whither then? I can't surmise.
Stinking and foul are my remains.
God save me when my body dies!

Index 1818. British Library, MS Harley 2316. Fourteenth century. Unique.

148

If man only thought
As well as he ought
Of that trip we abhor
From the bed to the floor,
And soon after it
From the floor to the pit,   *the grave*
And from pit into pain
That will evermore reign—
I believe that no sin
Should his heart ever win.

Index 1422. British Library, MS Arundel 292. Thirteenth century. Unique.

149

Where are they who went before
With horses, hounds, and hawks and more
To ride the fields and woods?
Or those rich ladies in their bowers

Decked out in gold for their short hours,
Amid their goods?

They ate and drank and had their day.
They lived glad lives in every way,
And men bowed low.
They held themselves apart and high,   10
Then in the twinkling of an eye,
Their souls did go.

Where are their laughter and their song,
Their stately trains that trailed along,
Their hawks and hounds?
All their joy is gone away;
Their weal is turned to "Welladay!"
Beneath the ground.

Their paradise was wasted here;
They lie in hell among their peers   20
In fire that slackens never.
Long is *aiee* and long is *oh*   *lamentations*
And long is *wei* and long is *wo*—
They won't return forever.

So then endure here, if you will,
Disease or hurt or other ill.
Forgo your comforts oft.
For though pain ranges every nerve,
Only think what you deserve,
And pain itself seems soft.   30

If that foul thing, the Devil,
Through bad advice or other evil
Has cast you down,
Rise up and fight him as before.
Stand, and vow you'll fall no more,
Nor fear his frown.

Take the Cross to be your staff,
And think, man, who in your behalf
Gave up His life!
He died for you; now pay Him back.   40
Seize the Cross and never slack
From holy strife.

Take up the shield of right belief,
While living in this vale of grief,
To arm your hand.
Fend off your foe with faith's sharp sword;
Combat the fiend for your reward—
That blessed land.

There you'll find day without a night,
Endless stores of strength and might,   50
Revenge on every foe.
You'll share God's everlasting life,
And holy peace, release from strife—
Joy evermore.

Maiden, mother, heaven's queen,
You're blessed with might; you've often been
Our shield against the wicked fiend.
Help us, lady, bring us clean
Before your Son, fit to be seen,
In heaven's bliss serene.   Amen.   60

Index 3310. Bodleian MS 1687. Thirteenth century. Not unique.

150 [14]

My wealth has faded like a show;
Nunc in pulvere dormio.   *"Now I sleep in dust." (burden)*

14. By James Ryman, a Franciscan friar of Canterbury.

I had riches; I had health;
I had honor, worldly wealth,
And yet death took me hence by stealth.
   Nunc in pulvere dormio.

Of happiness I had my will,
Of meat and drink I took my fill,
Yet death has lopped me with his bill.   *pruning hook*
   Nunc in pulvere dormio.

I had grace of form and face—
Was cosseted in every place—   10
Arrested now by death's cold mace,
   Nunc in pulvere dormio.

I had music, sweetest song,
And other games and mirth full long,
And yet death felled me with his prong.
   Nunc in pulvere dormio.

I had cunning, wisdom, wit.
Manhood, strength in me were knit.
Yet death has cast me in my pit.
   Nunc in pulvere dormio.   20

Oh, man of earth and all your kin,
Whose life is but a breath of wind,
Prepare your mind and put therein:
   Nunc in pulvere dormio.

While you are here, accept this guide;
It's not our lot to long abide.
You'll say with me, when you have died,
   Nunc in pulvere dormio.

Almighty God, now grant us grace
To profit by our time and space   30

Before we're thrust into this case:
Nunc in pulvere dormio.

Index 1298. Cambridge University MS Ee.1.12. Fifteenth century. Unique.

151[15]

Never was carrion so foul
As when man's pit becomes his cowl,
    Sunk in death, his life undone.
When death withdraws us one from another,
The sister will not know the brother,
    Nor will a father know his son.

Recorded in Penguin. Bodleian, MS Rawlinson C. 670. Fourteenth century. Not unique.

152

Winter wakens all my care.
Now that the trees are ragged and bare,
And sighs and mourning are my share,
    It often comes into my thought
    How this world's joys must come to naught.

We're happy now, and now are not,
As joy itself is clean forgot.
These words define our doleful lot:
    "All wears away but God's high will."
    We die, though we may take it ill.

All the seed I planted here
Dies unripened, dry and sere.
Jesus, make the truth shine clear.
    Dear Lord, shield my soul from hell.
    Die soon or live; no one can tell.

Index 4177. British Library, MS Harley 2253. Thirteenth century. Unique.

15. This poem appears in the *Fasciculus Morum,* a handbook for preachers.

153

There blows a cold wind today, today;
  The wind blows cold today.
Christ suffered His passion for man's salvation
  To keep the cold wind away.   *(burden)*

Our subjugation is called temptation.
  It rages night and day.
Remember, man, how Christ was slain
  To keep the cold wind away.

Sin's contortions, pride's extortions,
  Many do betray.
Say confession, make your profession,
  To keep the cold wind away.

Mary mild, for love of your child,
  Who died upon that day,   10
Be our salvation, avert damnation,
  To keep the cold wind away.

Our Lord was nailed, His life curtailed,
  Our ransom here to pay.
For our sins all they gave Him gall,
  To keep the cold wind away.

Such sins as sloth, whoring, oaths,
  Still chill the wind today.
Against those snares, He shook with cares
  To keep the cold wind away.   20

Oh man, remember the Lord so tender
  Who died, the harsh world's prey.
Pierced hands found rest upon His breast
  To keep the cold wind away.

Now pray with love to the King above
  Born without sin, I say,

Revere Him, then, with other men
    To keep the cold wind away.

At the hour of doom, freed from the tomb,
    When we meet on Judgment Day;   30
May Mary's son make us his own
    To keep the cold wind away.

There at the end, man, seek your friend,
    Embrace Him if you may.
The richest prize is Jesus Christ
    To keep the cold wind away.

Here let us end. Christ us defend;
    Be with us night and day.
Joys give us then none can amend,
    To keep the cold wind away.   40

Ringler MS Index 1674. Bodleian MS 7683. Sixteenth century. Unique.

154

Heaven is a precious tower.
Joy to those who heaven win.
Their bliss is more than heart can think;
Their mirth and ease will never end.

Sinful man, unless you mend,
Renouncing all your vice and sin,
Forever say, "Ach, welladay!"
For you shall never come therein.

Index 1179. National Library of Scotland, Advocates 18.8.1. Fourteenth century. Unique.

155

A God, and yet a man?
A maid, and yet a mother?
One wonders what wit can
Conceive this or the other.

A God—and can He die?
A dead man—can He live?
Say, what can wit reply?
What reason reason give?

God, truth itself, does teach it.
But our poor wit sinks under.
Mere reason cannot reach it.
Believe, and cease to wonder!

Index 37. Bodleian MS 11670. Fourteenth century. Unique.

156

Wretched man, why are you proud?
You're made of heavy earth, not air.
You came without a cloth or shroud;
No, you were born in want, and bare.

Think how when life has flown away,
And flesh is raked beneath the mould,
The corpse that minces proud today
Will fester, loathsome to behold.

Index 4239. Bodleian MS 1550. Fourteenth century. Not unique.

157

Lully, lullaye, lully, lullaye—
The falcon has borne my mate away.   *(burden)*

He bore him up; he bore him down;
He bore him to an orchard brown.

In that orchard is a hall.
Purple hangs from every wall.

And in that hall there is a bed,
Draped in shining gold and red.

In that bed there lies a knight,
His wide wounds bleeding day and night.

Beside the bed there kneels a maid.
Day and night she's wept and prayed.

Next to the bed there stands a stone,
With *Corpus Christi* writ thereon.   *"body of Christ"*

Ringler MS Index 530. Balliol College, Oxford, MS 354. Sixteenth century. Not unique.

Selections

FROM *THE VISION OF PIERS PLOWMAN*, B-TEXT[1]

WILLIAM LANGLAND

Piers Plowman, *an extended satire on English society, seems to have been a long-term undertaking of Langland (c. 1330–c. 1387). The poem exists in three versions, the A-, B-, and C-texts, and some scholars think another version once existed but has been lost. Although the C-text is generally believed to be Langland's latest, the B-text has long been preferred and most frequently reprinted. The poem was popular. It survives in more than fifty manuscript copies—not far removed from the eighty or so known manuscripts of* The Canterbury Tales.

While nothing is certain about Langland's life (or even his name, which may be fictitious), his poem seems to hint he was schooled around Malvern, a village in England's West Midlands, and later lived in London, where he may have supported himself by saying prayers for the dead. He represents himself as an outsider, a poor, dreamy fellow who nevertheless has a clear view of society's absurdities and injustices, which he presents with a unique mixture of humor and outrage. Langland's choice of the alliterative style of verse may be a deliberate indication of the distance he puts between himself and courtly poets like Chaucer and Gower.

The prologue that follows is a brief dream-vision Langland uses to introduce the rest of the poem, but it is a dream-vision of the world as he himself knew it, not a courtly allegory or other-worldly fantasy, and it pelts along fueled by his usual obsessive energy. As elsewhere in Piers Plowman, *transitions from one topic to the next are not always logical, adding to the poem's dreamlike effect, and the bulk of the people we meet are not nobles, kings, and queens but merchants, lying pilgrims, corrupt clergymen, frightened bureaucrats, and even cook-boys selling pies.*

---

1. Based on *The Vision of Piers Plowman*, ed. A. V. C. Schmidt. London and New York: Dent and E. P. Dutton, 1978.

THE PROLOGUE

In a summer season when soft was the sun
I swaddled myself in a smock, a seeming shepherd.
In this hermitlike habit, unholy of works,
I went wide through the world to hear of its wonders.
But on a May morning on the Malvern Hills[2]
A marvel befell me, by magic I thought.
I was weary of wandering and went down to rest
Under a broad bank by a brook's side.
While I lay there and leaned down and looked on the waters,
I slipped into sleep as the current slid by.   10
    Soon I was dreaming a marvelous dream:
There I was in a wilderness, not knowing where.
I looked to the east and on high in the sun
I saw a trim tower atop a tall hill
With a deep dale beneath and a dungeon therein
Amid deep and dark ditches, dreadful to see.
A fair field full of folk I found there between us,
All manner of men, the mean and the mighty,
Working and wandering as the world says they must.
    Some took up the plow and played only seldom.   20
In setting and sowing they sweated to garner
Winnings that gluttons soon waste with their greed.
Some pandered to pride with fine precious apparel;
In clouds of rich clothing those folk went concealed.
Many put themselves plainly to prayers and to penance,
For love of Our Lord these lived well and straight,
While hoping to have heaven's bliss at the last—
As anchorites and hermits[3] that hold to their cells,
Nor covet to carry themselves through the country,
For no lecherous lifestyle is likely to please them.   30

---

2. These high hills in England's West Midlands overlook a great stretch of placid farm-
land to the east and form a rugged shepherding area with a culture of its own.

3. Hermits lived in the wilderness. Anchorites closed themselves off in cells, often at-
tached to the walls of chapels or churches.

Some turned to trading, and these throve the better,
For it seems to our sight that such goods-sellers flourish.
Some would make mirth as minstrels must do.
They got gold by glee-singing, mostly guiltless I trust.
But jokers and janglers are Judas's children,
Feigning false fantasies, acting like fools,
Though they have ample wit to work well if they would.
Saint Paul's sanctions against such ones fill many a page,
But *qui loquitur turpiloquium* is Lucifer's lackey.   *"whoever speaks obscenities"*
    Beadsmen[4] and beggars buzzed about busily   40
Till their bags and their bellies were equally crammed,
Feigned hunger for alms there and fought over ale.
As gluttons, God knows, they go to their beds,
And rise up with ribaldry, the runagate robbers.
Sleeping and sloth beset this sort sorely.
    Pilgrims and palmers[5] gathered in parties
To seek out Saint James and the great saints of Rome.   *St. James's shrine at*
They went on their way with many wise tales . . .   *Compostella, in Spain*
And a license to lie all their lives ever after!
Some of them said they'd already sought saints.   50
Each tale that they told there was teeming with lies—
More falseness than fact as it seemed by their speech.
    A full helping of hermits with hook-headed staves
Wended toward Walsingham with wenches behind them—   *a pilgrim site*
Long, lanky louts who loathed honest work   *in England*
Hunched under hoods, to hold off from others.
They styled themselves hermits to go at their ease.
    I found friars as well, and from all the four orders.[6]
They preached to the people to profit themselves,
Glossing the Gospels any way that seemed good;   *interpreting, a*
To attain better trappings they twist God's word willfully.   *common charge*
Many such masters could buy what they would   *against friars*

---

4. Beadsmen were paid for saying prayers for some cause, usually dead souls. Langland
may have been a beadsman himself.

5. Palmers were pilgrims who had been to Jerusalem.

6. Franciscans, Dominicans, Carmelites, and Augustinians.

For their calling and commerce are closely commingled.
They plump up their purses pardoning lords,
And so several strange marvels beset us of late.
Unless they hold harder to God's holy church,
The worst woes in the world will come winging our way.
    A pardoner preached there with priestly pretensions.   *member of a minor*
He brought forth a bull[7] set with seals from a bishop   *order not permitted*
And proclaimed he himself might absolve guilty men   *to say Mass* 70
Of failures at fasting or falseness of faith.
Lewd men without learning liked well what he said
And came up to kneel by him, kissing his bull.
He rapped them with parchments, deluding their eyes.   *written indulgences*
The price of his pardons was pendants and rings.
Thus you give up your gold to satisfy gluttons.
You let it go lightly to unconstrained lechers!
If the bishop were blessed and believed as he should,
He'd not send his seal forth to dazzle the people.
But not just the bishop bears with their humbug: 80
The priest and the pardoner share silver as partners
That the poor of the parish should preserve for themselves.
    And yet parsons and priests would protest to their bishops
That tithes[8] had been poor since the time of the plague,   *the Black Death,*
Looking for licenses to linger in London   *1348–50*
And sing there for simony, for silver is sweet.   *collecting pay for Masses and prayers*
Bishops and bachelors, masters and doctors,   *graduates in divinity*
With charges from Christ and crowned with the tonsure[9]
(To show how they serve to shrive their parishioners
And preach to them, pray for them, feed up the poor),   90
Lay in London all Lent and at other times too.
Some serve the king by counting his coins.
In Exchequer and Chancery they call in his debts

---

    7. License to dispense papal indulgences. These were thought to reduce the time a sinner would spend in purgatory, not to absolve sins. They were not supposed to be sold, though they were often exchanged for gifts or money.

    8. Parishioners were supposed to tithe, that is, to pay a tenth of what they made to the church in money or goods.

    9. Clerical haircut featuring a bald crown circled by a fringe of hair.

From widows' estates and from orphans and waifs.
And some serve as servants to lords and their ladies.
Acting as stewards, they sit to hear suits.
Their Masses and Matins and most of their Hours   *canonical hours when set*
Are said only slackly. I fear at the last   *prayers were to be said*
Christ in his court will curse many of these.

    I perceived, too, the power Peter had in his keeping—   *traditionally the*
To bind and unbind,[10] as the Holy Book tells us—   *first pope*
How he left it with Love to the church on God's word.   *Matt. 16:19*
(Among four Cardinal Virtues,[11] the first of them all
Is Love, as men mention. These virtues indeed
Govern the gates of the heavenly kingdom.
Christ will close these to some, and show bliss there to others.)
But these cardinals[12] today who counsel the church,
Who presume to the power of appointing a pope—
The power of Saint Peter—I don't impugn them.
That election belongs to both learning and love,   110
So I can and yet cannot speak more of their court.[13]

    Then came a king with knights in his company.
The power of the people propped up his reign,
And with them Good Sense and whole crowds of his clerks
To counsel the king and save the poor commons.

    The king and his knights and the clergy as well
Chose that the commons should keep them well fed.
So the commons with Good Sense created all callings
And to profit the people ordained plowmen and such
To till and travail as the world's needs enjoined.   120
The king and the commons and Good Sense, the third,

10. The power of Peter, the first pope, to make or revoke declarations binding on earth
and in heaven.

11. St. Paul mentions three chief virtues—faith, hope, and love—and says that love is
the foremost (1 Cor. 13:13). Langland may have in mind a popular tradition identifying the
Cardinal Virtues as faith, hope, love, and charity.

12. "Princes of the Church"; they rank just below the pope and elect his successor, a non-
biblical power they assumed in the twelfth century.

13. This and several of the passages that follow are not very clear, perhaps because the
subjects were too dangerous to discuss openly in Langland's England.

Shaped laws and clear limits so each knew his own.[14]
   Then a lunatic looked up, a lean thing withal,   *Langland himself*
He knelt to the king and like a clergyman called:
"Christ keep thee, king, and thy kingdom as well,
And allow you to lead us as justice may guide you,
And for ruling us rightly may you be rewarded!"
   And then from the air a great angel of heaven
Called down in Latin (yea, for lesser men cannot
Urge or uphold their own rights for themselves,   130
But must suffer and serve). Thus said the angel:
"Sum Rex, sum Princeps; neutrum fortasse deinceps!
O qui iura regis Christi specialia regis,
Hoc quod agas melius, iustus est esto pius!
Nudum ius a te vestiri vult pietate.
Qualia vis metere, talia grana sere:
Si jus nudatur, nudo de iure metatur;
Si seritur pietas, de pietate metas."[15]
   Then railed a wanderer, reckless with words,
And to the angel on high this indigent answered: 140
"Dum rex a 'regere' dicatur nomen habere;
Nomen habet sine re nisi studet iura tenere."[16]
And next all the commons called out in Latin,
Counseling the king, construe it who will:
"Precepta regis sunt nobis vincula legis!"[17]
   With that, a rout of rats ran out at once
And mice along with them, more than a thousand.
They collected a council for common relief,

14. Langland is outlining the three "estates" of medieval society: the church (here Good Sense and all the learned professions); the nobility (the king and his knights and the ranks between them); and the commons, or peasantry. The church guides and informs society; the nobility defends it; and the commons work to feed it.

15. " 'I am king. I am prince,' you say. But soon you may be neither. O you who administer the laws of Christ, if you would do it better, be as merciful as you are just. Clothe naked justice with mercy. Sow as you hope to reap. If you strip justice naked, you will be tried by naked justice. If you sow mercy, you will be given mercy yourself."

16. "Yet a king is called a 'king' by reason of ruling; if he neglects the laws, he has the name of king but nothing else."

17. "The king's words are legal chains to us."

For a cat of the court came along when he liked
And pounced on them lightly, snatched them at will,   150
And played to their peril and pushed them about.
    "For dread," said the vermin, "we dare not look up!
If we grouch at his game he will grieve us all dearly,
Catch us or claw us, held close in his clutches,
So we'll loathe our own lives ere he lets us go free.
But might we by any means withstand his will,
We'd be lofty as lords are and live at our ease."
    A rat of renown, one most ready of tongue,
Set forth a solution as he himself saw it:
"I've seen creatures," said he, "in the city of London   160
With colorful collars clasped round their necks,
Some craftily fashioned.[18] They are left without leashes.
In warrens or wastelands they go as they will.
The same is true elsewhere as I have heard tell.
If a bell could be bound to this cat by a collar,
One might know where he went and straight run away!
Therefore," said the rat, "my thinking runs thus:
We must buy us a bell of brass or bright silver
To clench on a collar for our common cause
And clamp on the cat. Aye, for then we can hear   170
Where he rests or he rambles and runs in his play.
And if playfulness pleases him, we may come out,
Appear in his presence, and play as we can.
But, beware! If he's angry we'll bide far away."
    The whole race of rats accepted this reasoning—
But when the bright bell was bought and clipped to the collar,
No rat in the rout for the whole realm of France
Would brave the bold cat to buckle it on!
Not all England itself could entice them to try.
They called themselves cowards and feeble of counsel   180
And allowed that their labor and study were lost.
    A mouse of much learning, or so I thought then,
Sternly strode forth and stood watching them all.

---

18. Langland probably meant gold chains worn by officials as well as collars on dogs and cats.

To the council of vermin he ventured advice:
"Say we killed this cat, sirs. Why, another would come
To claw all our kind though we crept under benches.
So I counsel our commonwealth: let the cat be.
We must never act boldly and show him the bell.
While he runs after rabbits, he won't rend our flesh,
For then finer meats feed him. So don't flout him like fools: 190
Better a sharp loss than long-lasting sorrow.
We'd be caught in confusion if we escaped from this cat,
For I heard my sire say, only seven years since:
'Where the cat is a kitten, the court will be smitten.'
And Holy Writ witnesses, read it who will:
'Ve terrae ubi puer rex est, etc.'[19]
No man may rest there for rats in the night.
For many a man's malt would we small mice destroy,
And you wretched rats would ruin many men's clothes,
Except that a cat of the court kept you cowed.   200
If you rats had your will you'd be rash and unruly.
    "As for me," said the mouse, "I here vouch for my vision:
Neither cat nor yet kitten shall be grieved by my counsel.
No more carping of collars that cost me full little
(And if they had cost me, I'd tell no one now!)
But suffer the cat to clutch such as he can—
Coupled, uncoupled, catch all that he may.
And I warn all wise vermin: watch out for yourselves."
    (What this story may show, you men who are merry
Work out without me, for I will not say more!)   210
    Then a hundred hove forward in hoods made of silk—
Sergeants they seemed to me, serving the bar,   *i.e., barristers*
Pleading for pennies and pounding the law.
No love of the Lord ever loosened their lips—
As soon measure mist among Malvern's high hills
As make those men mumble without showing money.
Barons and burghers and bondsmen as well

---

19. "Woe to the land where the king is a child!" (Eccl. 10:16). Richard II was only ten years old when he became king in 1377. Langland's fable reflects the regency of John of Gaunt and his conflicts with the houses of Lords (the rats) and Commons (the mice).

I saw there assembled as you shortly will hear.
Bakers and brewers and butchers abounded;
With a wellspring of weavers of wool, and of linen;   220
Tailors and tinkers and market tax-takers;
Masons and miners and myriad others.
Of all kinds of laborers some lingered there,
Such as ditchers and diggers that do their work ill
And dribble their days out in bawdy, bad ballads.
Cooks and their cook-boys out calling, "Hot pies!
Good geese and pork! Go, we dine, go we!"
Tapsters and taverners touted their wares:
"White wine of Gascony, wine of Alsace!
Wine of the Rhine and Rochelle for your roast!"   230
All this I saw sleeping, and seven times more.

FROM *CONFESSIO AMANTIS*

JOHN GOWER

John Gower (c. 1330–1408) wrote in three different languages, one or two of which, he must have reasoned, might survive. His Latin and French poems expose the faults of English society under Richard II. Confessio Amantis *(The Lover's Confession) is a courtly anthology of more than 140 stories from various sources, mostly about love. Despite the Latin title, the poem is in English, and since it was written around 1390, it may show the influence of Chaucer, much of whose English verse had already appeared by then. Chaucer may also have inspired Gower's relative lightness of tone. As Gower says in his prologue, the work combines "somewhat of lust, somewhat of lore."*

Amans, the lover, is Gower himself. When he complains to Venus about his lack of success, she hands him over to her priest Genius, who tells the stories recounted in the collection to correct the poet's misconceptions and faults. By the end of the work, Gower has heard enough. He's too old to be a lover anyway, so he retires from the field. Though the stories in the work are supposed to exemplify the seven deadly sins, love is the real sustaining issue, and Gower pursues it with a delicate touch. Like Ovid, the source of many of his tales, Gower is attuned to the feelings of women and treats them with special sympathy. Alcyone, his protagonist in the following story, is no exception.

THE TALE OF CEYX AND ALCYONE[1]

I read once in a piece of poetry   *Ovid, Metamorphoses, XI*
How Ceyx, a king in Thessaly,
Took Alcyone for his wife.
She loved him as she loved her life.
He had a brother, too, whose name,
Dedalion, was known to fame.
You see, that prince was changed one day
From manlike shape, in some strange way,

1. Pronounced SEE-iks and Al-SEE-on-ee.

Into a hawk. This transformation
Filled Ceyx' mind with grave consternation   10
And fired a longing in his heart
To make a journey, sail apart
Into a strange and distant place
Where pilgrims traveled seeking grace.
There he would sacrifice and pray
To learn if he might find a way
To move the gods to grant his plea
And set his transformed brother free—
Restore his form, so once again
The world might see him as a man.   20
Now, to this purpose, without fail,
The king prepared himself to sail,
Fitting out his waiting ship.
To see him off upon his trip,
His wife came with him to the shore,
And there the heartsick queen implored
The king to comfort her and say
How long he meant to be away.
"Two months or less," was his best guess.
Then leaving her among the rest,   30
He took his leave and forth he sailed.
His forlorn lady wept and wailed
Before they led home at last.
But when those same two months had passed
Of Ceyx's absence, as you heard,
And still his queen had had no word,
She thought she knew all care could teach.
Her worries made the queen beseech
The gods who rule the distant skies.
But Juno most in sacrifice   *queen of the gods*
The sorrowing Thracian queen petitioned
To save her husband and his mission
Or say at least how Ceyx fared.
Her pain was such that Juno heard
And swiftly sent her messenger
Iris,[2] by name, to act for her:

---

2. Iris, the goddess of the rainbow, carried messages from heaven to earth.

To Somnus' house the nymph must fly   *god of sleep*
And raise a dream to satisfy
The queen's obsession, make her know
How Ceyx did, for weal or woe.   50
    Thus Iris left the airy stage
From whence she flits as Juno's page,
Wrapped inside her rainy cape,
Which shimmered down its trailing shape
With all the hues the world can show—
A hundred more than humans know.
The heavens' light in one smooth arc
The goddess bent into the dark,
To where the god of sleep is found,
A curious country all around.   60
Cimmeria is not far away,   *darkness, part of the underworld*
And there, it says in poetry,
Somnus keeps his house in state—
A wondrous pile, and no debate.
It's in a cave beneath a hill
Where no sun shines nor ever will.
There men can never tell aright
What is day and what is night.
They keep no fire there, strong or weak,
No door to let in light or creak   70
And start a sleepy eye awake,
But all's arranged for slumber's sake.
And, speaking next of what's without,
No great, tall trees stand round about
Where cawing crows or raucous pies   *magpies*
Can perch and freight the air with cries.
There dwells no cock to crow in day
Or beast to bawl in any way.
The hillside stretches all around,
And growing widely on the ground   80
Are poppies, in whose seeds lies sleep.
Drowsy herbs crowd thick and deep.
A smooth stream laps in quiet tones
Upon a bank of little stones.
Lethe is that river's name.

It drowns itself but not its fame
In Somnus' cave where all things sleep.
All these delights does Somnus keep
Around his house. As for the bed
Within his chamber, I've heard said   90
Its boards are all of ebony,
The dark wood of a drowsy tree.
Then to ensure the god sleeps soft,
Upon a feather bed aloft
He lies in pillows made of down.
His room is thickly scattered round
With dreams strewn by the thousandfold.
Thus Iris came to Somnus' hold,
And by his bedside, black and dark,
She spoke the words that he must mark—   100
The message she was sent to bear—
Relaying Juno's orders there.
It took her several tries to dent
His sleep and tell him what she meant,
But at the last, although he grouched,
Sleep reared himself up from his couch,
And pledged to her, "It shall be so."
And then out from a thousand more
Who lay about his house asleep
He chose three figures from the heap   110
To craft a dream as Juno said.
The first of these, as I have read,
Was Morpheus, who has the skill
To take on any form he will,
The shape of any man or maid.
This gives him power, oft displayed,
Of shaping visions that seem true.
Ithecus was chosen too.
Of every voice he has the sound.
He knows the semblance and the ground   120
Of every life, just as it is.
The third selected after this
Was Panthasas. That sprite can shift
The firmest shape, such is his gift,

Transform it to another kind.
Now these three spirits, as I find,
Control the substance of all dreams.
In some they make things what they seem;
In others everything's a joke.
Well, Morpheus, of whom I spoke,   130
When it was night appeared alone
Unto this queen as one well known.
He seemed the king she loved before,
But tossed up dead upon the shore.
How it was he perished there
The others showed her for their share:
The tall, tempestuous black cloud,
The maddened sea, winds howling loud,
All this she dreamed, and saw him die.
She called out when his death was nigh   140
(Though she still lay asleep in bed).
Awakened by her cry of dread,
Her women rose and crowded near,
Frightened by their lady's fear.
Alarmed, they asked her how she fared,
And she told what she'd seen and heard—
Her dream, that is—in each detail.
They glossed it as a hopeful tale
And said the vision tokened good.
But till the queen knew how things stood   150
She banished comfort from her heart.
When morning broke she went apart
Toward the sea, to where she'd dreamed
The body lay. Drawn on, it seemed,
She went toward the billows' sound.
There, spraddled dead, her lord she found,
Floating in the heaving froth.
Her wits were scattered, by my troth,
And she, who feared no danger now,
Leaped forth into the ocean's maw.   160
To clasp the king was all her will.
    This cursed day of double ill
The gods who rule the skies above

Beheld and, for the truth of love
In which this worthy lady stood,
Sent down their power upon the flood.
They brought her and her lord as well
Back to life amid the swell—
But now refashioned into birds!
Both rode upon the waves, I heard;   170
And when she saw her lord again
Alive, afloat, and free of pain,
And she a bird of his own sort,
The queen swam after him in sport.
She felt a joy that banished dread.
She went to him with wings outspread,
And as her form allowed her to
She kissed him as she used to do,
And sheltered him, now freed of harms,
With folded wings in place of arms.   180
And though her beak was hard, not soft,
She billed with him as she had oft,
And found despite her birdlike form
That she could love him and perform
All the pleasance of a wife
As well as in their other life—
For though she'd lost that shape she bore,
Her will stood as it had before:
To serve him sweetly as she might.
Thus even now by day or night   190
They live upon the sea as one,
Where many a daughter, many a son,
They've brought forth of their birdish kind.
And so that men may hold in mind
Alcyone, the faithful queen,
Her birds are known where they are seen
As Halcyons,[3] the lady's name.

3. This name is now associated with the kingfishers, the family *Alcedinidae,* but Ovid and Gower must have meant sea birds, perhaps some type of gulls. The ancients believed that halcyons nested at sea (though no bird does) and were able to calm the ocean while their eggs were incubating.

FROM *THE SQUIRE* OF *LOW DEGREE*

In this sporadically likeable poem, probably from the mid-fifteenth century, the Princess of Hungary falls in love with a common squire, promising him her hand when he can better his state in life. Before long, however, the squire is imprisoned and presumed dead by the grieving princess, who is so heartsick that for the next seven years she keeps what she thinks are his remains in a sarcophagus next to her bed.

In the selection below the king tries to jolly his daughter into a better state of mind through an exaggerated list of pleasures she can enjoy, an agreeable reminder of the pageantry, feasts, and fancy dress the Middle Ages held dear. This catalog of delights is also a highly accomplished piece of verse—smooth, sophisticated tetrameter couplets that place the work well up among the courtlier examples of Middle English metrical romance.

"Tomorrow hunting you shall fare,
And ride, my daughter, in a chair,
Upholstered in bright velvet red,
With cloth of gold about your head
And damask, white and azure blue,
Embroidered well with lilies new.
Your trappings will bear knobs of gold
And chains enameled many fold.
Your cloak will be, unless I err,
Of crimson cloth and ermine fur.   10
Spanish horses, small and white,
Will draw you, draped in trappings bright,
And you'll have harps and lutes and song
To please you as you go along.
You'll have malmsey and Greek wine,   *costly drinks*
Hippocras and Mountrose fine,
Antioch, piment, muscatel,
Clary, garnard, and Rochelle.

Red wine your taste will rectify,
With pots of Alsace standing by.   20
You'll have venison and bacon,
The finest fowl that may be taken,
A leash of greyhounds, too, to strike   *i.e., three greyhounds*
Deer and other game alike.
You'll be seated on a stand
Where stags and does come to your hand.
All your dreary airs will go
When once the silver bugles blow.
Small hounds will mill about the place,
While seven score big ones lead the chase.   30
Then homeward, daughter, you will ride,
Hawking along the river's side,
With goshawks, merlins, and their kin:
Gyrfalcons, hobbies, peregrines.   *kinds of hawks*
    "Once at home, among your men,
You'll have songs and dances then.
Little children, without fail,
Will sing to you like nightingales.
And then it's off to Evensong   *a religious service*
While trilling trebles trail along.   40
Your priests will all wear damask bright,
Well set with pearls to catch the light—
The altar spread with precious cloth
And brocade hems to set it off.
Your incense burners will be gold
With blue enamel in each fold.
The organ will swell and choirs chant,
With counterpoint and smooth descant.
    "And then you'll go outside to sup
In tented arbors well set up   50
With tapestries upon the grounds,
And colored gems and diamonds.
A cloth of gold will crown your head,
And peacocks set with jewels of red.
Your men will bring you all you wish,
A fresh delight in every dish!

The nightingale, upon its thorn,[1]
Will sing for you both night and morn.
A hundred knights in your control
Shall talk to you or dance or bowl.   60
Unhappiness will fly away
As you watch pools of fish at play,
Then walk your arbors and your grounds,
Through garden paths of great renown.
   "To a bridge you'll come anon
Fashioned well of wood and stone.
Next, a barge shall heave in sight
With twenty-four oar blades flashing bright,
And trumpeters and clarions,
To ride the water up and down.   70
Then to the salt sea, flecked with foam,
To see your manor far from home,
With eighty ships of fighting men;
And barges, too, on every hand;
And carracks—sails upon each mast—
To split the waves and tame the blasts;
With galleys good upon the water—
Eighty oars apiece, my daughter.
The men shall sing as forth they row:
'Hey now! How now! Here we go!'   80
Once at sea, you'll call for wine
In precious cups with spices fine,
Gentle pots of ginger green,
With dates and dainties fit for queens;
Forty torches burning bright
Upon the bridge will cast their light.
   "Lo, now they bring you to your berth
With smiles and laughter, tender mirth.
Your drapes are garnished, white and blue,
With marigolds and lilies too.   90
Silken curtains fall in folds,
Bedposts made of solid gold.

---

1. Nightingales were said to press against thorns to make their song more sweet.

The canopy above your head
Shows popinjays of white and red.
Your quilts are furred with ermine white
With golden stitching, fine and tight.
Each blanket is the finest wool;
Your linen sheets are smooth and cool.
Then too, above your bed so soft,
A golden cage shall hang aloft,   100
A nest of herbs and heated spices
Bought far or near at any prices.
Frankincense and olibanum   *aromatics*
Will sweetly burn to scent the room.
If sleep holds off and you must wake,
So will your minstrels, for your sake. . . ."
   "I thank you, father, but you see,
None of this appeals to me."

From Virgil's *Aeneid*, Book II

Gavin Douglas

*Gavin Douglas (c. 1476–1522), a clergyman and son of Archibald Douglas,
fifth Earl of Angus, rose to become Bishop of Dunkeld in 1516. He was also a
notable writer in his Scottish dialect. His dream-allegory* The Palice of Honour *devotes more than two thousand lines to describing honor—represented as
a palace ruled by Dame Venus—and cataloging the heroes, lovers, and poets
who deserve to receive it.*

    Douglas is better known, though, for his 1513 translation of Virgil's Aeneid,
*a work that inaugurated a long and rich tradition of classical translations in
English. Douglas's pentameter couplets do a remarkably good job of rendering
Virgil's Latin, especially in rousing passages concerning battle and storms.*

    *For some reason, Douglas divided each of Virgil's books into chapters, each
beginning with its own brief summary. What follows is Chapter 6 of Book II,
where Aeneas describes how he awoke to find Greek invaders roaming inside
Troy and began his whirlwind journey into the heart of the falling city.*

Chapter 6

*How Aeneas the Greeks' treason did perceive
And what debate he made his city to relieve.*

Throughout the city rose the din of war,
A whisper first, but ever more and more,
And clearer waxed the rumor and the sound,
Till even in my father's house and grounds,
Well ringed with trees, secluded by the way,
So busy grew the turmoil of the fray
And rattlings of armor in the street,
I woke in fright and started to my feet.   10
High up to the roof I climbed alone
And strained my ears there, standing still as stone.

A rustling sort of noise reached me at last
As when a fire, before the fell wind's blast,
Sweeps down the field where grain stands rank on rank,
Or when a stream in spate hurls down its bank
Or finds a gap through which to foam and flood,
Riving red earth and running dark with mud
To drown men's crops—the work of plows—at once,
And drive before it trees and stones and stumps.   20
The helpless herdsman sees the grisly sight
From some tall pinnacle or craggy height,
And stands uncertain, doubting what it means,
Abashed by sounds and prodigies he's seen.
Just so, I then, by every sign and clue
Discerned the Greeks, and all their falsehood knew.
Their hidden plans were now laid bare to us.
Nearby, the lodging of Deïphobus   *a Trojan prince*
Collapsed in flames and fanned the fires it spawned
To burn another house, Ucalegon's.   30
Beyond the town, the waves off Sigeum's coast   *promontory near Troy*
Gleamed bright with fires lit by the Achaean host.   *the Greek invaders*
The rising cries of men and trumpets' blasts,
Drove me half mad. I armed myself full fast,
Though arms were vain. I'd try, although I'd fail,
If any force of mine could yet prevail.
Hand to hand to hurtle through the fight
With other Trojans, ravening through the night,
To reach the palace, that was our desire.
The fury licked our minds with maddening fire,   40
So that we thought it seemly in the field
To die in battle, each beneath his shield.
But lo! Here Panthus came amid the spears,
Othriades' son, and one who had for years
Been Trojans' strength and Phoebus's holy priest.
Beneath his arm and folded to his breast,
He held his relics and—despite all odds—
The salvaged figures of our vanquished gods!
Not far behind him, slipping as he ran,
He drew his little grandson by the hand,   50

Fleeing like a madman through the crowd.
"Panthus! Stay! What news?" I called aloud.
"How did you leave your temple and its gear?
To what remaining fortress must we steer?"
These words were scarcely out when piteously
The priest raised up his voice to answer me:
"The day has come," he said, "for Troy to end,
A mortal fate no wailing may amend.
We once were Trojans, lived in Ilium,   *Troy*
But now the light of Phrygia is gone.   60
Fierce Jupiter has given all to Greece!
The city falls in flames through his caprice.
The Greeks are now our lords, despite our force.
Inside the city walls their hollow horse
Spews armored men, while false Sinon,[1]
Now hailed as victor, eggs the flames along,
Sets new fires gladly, as if it were a sport.
At either gate there swarm by good report
A thousand Greeks. They rove the town in clusters.
Some companies with spears and lances muster   70
To set a watch where lanes and alleys meet,
While parties armed with swords roam every street.
All through the town they ravish, stab, and slay.
Our hapless guards who held the gates today
Could scarce defend themselves, try as they might.
The Fates destroyed them quickly in the fight."
Spurred on by Panthus and the gods' behest,
Amid the flames and armored men I pressed,
Rushing always where the Furies called
Or where noise drew me—where the battle bawled   80
And war's worst clamors rose into the air.
Then of my fellow Trojans came two pairs:
Ripheus first, beneath the shining moon;
His brave companion Epytus followed soon.
Hypanis next with Dymas came in haste
To join our side. Along with us they paced.

1. Greek spy who persuaded the Trojans to bring the horse inside their city walls.

And Mygdon's son as well, young Coroebus,
To serve his love as fate had ruled he must.
Cassandra brought him to the Trojan corps   *a princess who had*
To help her father, Priam, in the war.   *foreseen the fall of Troy*
Unfortunate! He disbelieved what she,
His chosen spouse, had said in prophesy.
Now when I saw these warriors form a band,
All ready to strike Greeks at my command,
I stopped a space and said as they drew near:
"You strong young men, my friends who join me here,
With stalwart hearts and courage worth renown,
In vain you rush to rescue our doomed town;
See how it burns! See the red flames race!
The gods of Troy themselves have quit the place.   100
They helped our empire stand strong in its day,
But now their shrines lie empty, left for prey.
Vow that your hearts are firm, and uncoerced
You mean to follow me through this and worse.
You see our fortune. All things go awry.
There is no more. Together we will die.
So now among these foemen let us thrust.
To vanquished folk it's comforting and just
To have no hope of victory in view."
In spite of what I said, their courage grew.   110
They ranged with me as wolves who know no laws,
Whom the blind fury of their empty maws
Drives from their dens to make all things their prey,
And feed their hungry whelps as best they may.
Although the Greeks ringed round, we took the field,
Intent to strike back hard and never yield.
Along the foremost streets we made our way,
But prowling where the darkest shadows lay.

Narratives

THE LAND OF COCKAYNE[1]

Written in Ireland in the second half of the thirteenth century, this poem, composed in surprisingly smooth couplets, recalls alternate-world fictions going back to the second-century satirist Lucian, who described a fantasy trip to the moon. The name Cockayne *has never been fully explained. It may derive from a German term for cake. The word crops up in France and elsewhere in connection with never-ending foodstuffs and easy, guiltless sex. Here the tradition is adapted into a genial satire (or perhaps just wishful thinking) concerning monastic life. Another variation on the same theme appears three hundred years later in Pieter Bruegel's painting* The Land of Cockayne.

Out in the sea far west of Spain,
There lies a country called Cockayne.
No other land beneath the sky
Can match that place, or even try.
Though Paradise is choice and bright,
Cockayne, sirs, is a fairer sight,
For what is there in Paradise
But grass and flowers and cloudless skies?
While heaven's joys are wide and sweet,
There's nothing there but fruit to eat.   10
There is no bower, bench, or hall
And only water to drink withal.
People? There are only two:
Elijah and Enoch,[2] good sirs, who
Forlorn and desolate must go.
They live alone, forever so.

---

1. This poem comes from the Franciscan abbey at Kildare, Ireland. It may be a satire on rival abbeys, or the gray and white abbeys it mentions may correspond to the Carmelite (white) and the Franciscan (gray) abbeys in Kildare itself. The end of the poem sounds a bit like an appeal for indulgence from the hearers, who might have been the Franciscan friars, enjoying a little foolery directed at themselves.

2. These two were carried alive into heaven. Everyone else there is a spirit, with only spiritual needs.

But Cockayne swims with drink and meat;
You needn't work there, only eat.
The meat is choice; the drink is clear
At every meal all through the year.   20
I tell you true, for joy and mirth,
Cockayne goes by itself on earth.
No province, town, or earthly land
Holds so much bliss on every hand.
    That place shows many welcome sights.
It's always daytime, never night.
They have no feuds or other strife,
No death at all, but only life.
There's no lack there of meat or cloth,
Not a man or woman wroth.   30
There is no serpent, wolf, or fox,
Horse or nag or cow or ox.
There is no sheep or goat or swine,
No filth or stink of any kind.
No locked stable, barn, or stall;
The land is open, free to all.
There is no flea or fly or louse
In cloth or town or bed or house.
There is no thunder, sleet, or hail,
No crawling worm, no slimy snail.   40
No storms they have deserve the name.
No man or woman blind or lame,
But all is glee and joy and game.
Happy are they who taste the same!
There are rivers, great and fine,
Of milk and honey, oil and wine.
Water's used for nothing there
But washing up and combing hair.
They have every kind of fruit,
And joy and love without dispute.   50
    They have an abbey—what a sight!—
Of holy monks, both gray and white.
Among its cloisters, bowers, and halls,
Cornish pasties form the walls,

Filled with lovely fish and meat,
The tastiest you'll ever eat.
Flapjack shingles cover all:
Church and cloister, bower and hall.
The pegs are puddings, rich and fat,
Kingly treats for all of that.   60
Don your bib and eat along.
Suit yourself; you can't go wrong.
All is free to young and old:
The stout, the stern, the meek, the bold.
    The abbey cloister, fair and light,
Broad and long (a seemly sight),
Is ringed with costly crystal piles,
With precious stones along the aisles.
Each column, sirs, about the place
Is coral-topped and jasper-based.   70
    In one meadow stands a tree;
Ah! What a sight that is to see!
With galingale and ginger roots,   *aromatic spices*
And fragrant nutmegs on each shoot.
Fine coriander forms the flower;
Its cinnamon bark could scent a bower.
Cloves for fruit upon each twig;
And dangling peppers, ripe and big!
There are acres of red roses
And lilies, sweet to eyes and noses.   80
These never wither, day or night.
By heaven, that's a noble sight!
    Four wells rise, serene and calm:
One of treacle; one of balm;
One of lotion; one of wine—
Each one running all the time.
Beneath each stream its golden bed
Is paved with jewels, green and red,
With sapphire stars and cabochons,
Pearls and rubies, for the nonce,   90
Emeralds, zircons, and at last,
Beryl, onyx, clear topaz,

Amethyst and chrysolite,
Chalcedony and hepatite.
  Birds abound. They never fail:
Throstles, thrushes, nightingales—
The oriole, the chanting lark,
And many more of equal mark.
These seldom stop but spend their might
In merry singing, day and night.   100
  Moreover, I must not omit it,
Preroasted geese, each neatly spitted,
Fly to that abbey to be caught
And call in coming, "Geese, all hot!"
With their own garlic sauce they come,
Deftly seasoned, all and some.
Their larks, I own, are widely known,
And fly to men—each gets his own.
From vast stew pots they rise in droves,
Well dressed with cinnamon and cloves.   110
Getting drink requires no speech;
All he likes comes free to each.
When the monks go in to Mass,
Windows made of colored glass
Turn themselves to crystal bright
To give the monks below more light.
When Mass is over for the day
And all the books are put away,
The glass transforms from clear and plain,
Goes back again, resumes its stain.   120
  The young monks are released each day:
After meat they go to play.
No hawk or fowl that goes on high
Flitters faster through the sky
Than those young monks go look for fun.
Their sleeves and hoods flap as they run!
When the abbot sets them free,
He himself enjoys their glee;
But nonetheless he warns the throng,
They must return for Evensong.   *vespers, at sunset*   130

The monks run on without a care,
Rushing here and everywhere.
Now, sirs, when the abbot sees
Not one stops but onward flees,
He takes a maid to be his drum,
Turns her up to show her bum,
And beats her buttocks with his hand
To make the monks heed his command.
With that, the rowdy monks are stayed—
Drawn back there by the abbot's maid.   140
They gather round as he designed
And they themselves pat her behind—
And then, worn out by all their play,
Wend meekly home to end their day.
They make a pretty sight, I think,
Returning to their meat and drink.
    Another abbey stands nearby
In truth, a fair, great nunnery,
Up a river of sweet milk
Whose banks are paved with precious silk.   150
When days are hot, the young nuns vote
To take their leisure in a boat
And down the river guide their course
With their rudders and their oars.
Then when they're far enough away,
They strip themselves full bare to play,
And leap at once into the stream
To swim there in the running cream.
The young monks watch the swimming place.
When nuns are there, why, down they race.   160
They come among the nuns anon,
And every monk selects his one.
They quickly bear their pretty prey
Back to their rooms, not far away,
And teach the nuns a special prayer
With spraddled legs raised in the air!
The monk who'd be a stallion good,
An able man beneath his hood,

Can find himself, sirs, never fear,
A dozen new wives every year.   170
They're his to take; no need to ask.
Each carries out her loving task.
Meanwhile, the monk who sleeps the best,
Who gives himself to quiet rest,
There's hope for him, by God I swear,
That he'll soon be an abbot there.
   Whoever hopes to see that place
Must suffer long to heap up grace.
Seven years in pig manure
He must wade, my lords, for sure,   180
Sunk in ordure to the chin,
Before he'll ever come therein.
   My good lords, you're kind, I know.
I hope you stay with us below
Unless, sirs, you can find a way
To do this penance, as I say;
But then may you enjoy this land,
Enter there and not be banned.
All pray to God that this may be!
Amen, my lords, for charity!   190

SIR ORFEO

As its anonymous fourteenth-century author informs us, this story is a Breton
lai, *a type of narrative poetry associated with Brittany and with older Celtic
traditions and folklore. In Breton lais highborn heroes or heroines (the form is
less gender-bound than most medieval poetry) search for love against a back-
ground of magic and fairy lore.*

*The lai's most famous exponent was Marie de France, a twelfth-century An-
glo-Norman poet who lived and worked at least part of her life in England.
Like Marie's lais,* Sir Orfeo *may have been meant to be sung to a harp ac-
companiment, though it sounds more like a popular poem than a court enter-
tainment. Although the poem has no known source, many have guessed it is
based on a lost French original. The story shows considerable ingenuity in con-
verting Thrace into Winchester, the Greek poet Orpheus into a medieval king,
and the dismal realm of Pluto into an alternate world of fairies and
changelings. The poem's happy ending is another medieval adaptation.*

Sir Orfeo *seems to have been widely known, for it appears in three manu-
scripts—one from Scotland—produced over a period of a hundred years or
more. Chaucer may have read it and possibly echoed Orfeo's visions of the fairies
in the magic illusions of his "Franklin's Tale," which is itself a Breton lai. The
poem's catalog of dead and maimed figures may also have influenced the Tem-
ple of Mars section of "The Knight's Tale."*

Men read tales of long ago,
Stories that the wise clerks know,
Lays men used to harp and sing,
Noble tales of wondrous things:
Some of weal; some of woe;
Joy and mirth, both high and low.
Some of treachery and guile,
Strange happenings of every style;
Some of ribaldry and jokes,
Or magic glens and fairy folks.   10
Of everything a man may know,
Great or little, swift or slow,

The Breton poets made their lays.[1]
What they heard to blame or praise
In tales and stories of the past,
They put in verse so it might last.
Whenever they might hear a tale
Of any portent, good or ill,
They took their harps and rhymed the same—
Supplied it meter and a name.   20
Among the stories they recall,
I know a few, though hardly all.
So hark now, lords, before we go,
And I shall tell of Orfeo.

   Sir Orfeo was king here once,
In our fair England, for the nonce.
No man was hardier than he,
Handsome, courteous, and free.
His father came from King Pluto,
His mother rose from King Juno,[2]   30
And both forebears were held divine
For deeds remembered from their times.
This Orfeo, as tales agree,
Loved harping well and minstrelsy.
No good performers came his way
But he would welcome them to stay.
He himself could play the harp—
His hands were fleet; his wits were sharp.
He practiced so, the able man,
No finer harper graced the land.   40
No one could be where Orfeo was
And hear his harp without applause.
No, everyone who heard him play
Was soon transported far away
To taste the joys of Paradise!

---

1. Not very accurate. Breton lais are usually courtly and polite and generally concern Arthurian and other Celtic-flavored stories of noble characters. Fairies are common, but not ribaldry and jokes.

2. The writer is a bit muddled. Juno, of course, was a goddess. She was Jupiter's wife.

His harp strings raised them to the skies.
From Traciens[3] this king once reigned,
A fortress city, well maintained.
(This Traciens town still stands, I vow,
But it is called Winchester now.)   50
The king had wed a queen of price,
A lovely one called Heurodis,[4]
The fairest lady in their day
Of all who went in fine array—
A font of joy and love and duty,
No words could even touch her beauty.

It happened at the start of May
When days are hot and hearts are gay,
And there's an end to winter showers,
And every field is full of flowers,   60
And blossoms burst from every tree,
And all is mirth as men may see,
It fell that Heurodis, the queen,
Led forth two maidens, fair and clean,
And went to spend her morning hours
Beside an orchard ringed with flowers.
She longed to see the blossoms spring
And hear the gentle songbirds sing.
And there they sat them down, all three,
Beneath a grafted orchard tree.[5]   70
It wasn't long before the queen
Fell fast asleep upon the green.
The maidens dared not waken her
But let her sleep. She didn't stir
But slept until the noon hour passed

3. Thrace was a region, not a city, associated with ancient Greece. Here it is naturalized as an English town—the royal city of Winchester, seat of Alfred the Great and capital of England until after the Norman Conquest.

4. Eurydice, in the Greek myth. The poet seems to have pronounced the name UR-o-DICE or HUR-o-DICE.

5. The fact that the tree was grafted, an "ympe-tree," and therefore unnatural seems important.

And morning slipped away at last.
    But, lo, the moment she awoke
She screamed and gagged as if she choked.
She wrung her hands and thrashed her feet
And scratched her visage, soft and sweet.   80
She tore her robes, before, behind.
She seemed a thing without a mind.
The pair of maidens by her side,
Far too startled to abide,
Raced to the palace in their fright
And quickly told each squire and knight
The queen was mad, and as her men
They must help them bring her in.
The knights all ran, and ladies too;
More than sixty damsels flew,   90
Hastening to save the queen.
They took her up and wiped her clean
And bore her to her own soft bed
And covered her and held her head.
But she could only shriek and pray
And thrash about to be away.
    Orfeo, who heard of this,
Thought nothing worse could go amiss.
He brought his own knights, brisk and keen,
To stay with him and watch the queen,   100
And when he saw her there, he said:
    "O sweetheart, have your senses fled?
You've always been so calm and still,
But now you're shrieking, harsh and shrill.
Your body, dear, so smooth and white,
You rip yourself as if in spite!
Your sweet complexion, warm and hale,
Is ghastly looking, wan and pale.
Your fingers, dear one—fine and good—
Are loathsome now, red with your blood.   110
Alas! Your pretty, lovesome eyes!
They stare at me in mad surmise
As if I were your foe! Ah me!

Darling, let this crying be.
Just tell me what is wrong and how,
My dearest, I can help you now."
　The lady's thrashing stilled at last
Though sobs still wracked her hard and fast.
She spoke, although her voice was low:
"Alas, my lord, Sir Orfeo! 120
Ever since I've been with you
We've been as one, sir, kind and true.
You have meant my life to me
And I to you, as I could see.
But now we shall be forced apart.
For I must go away, dear heart!"
　"Alas," he said, "abandon me?
Why and where? Are you not free?
Where you go, dear, there I shall be,
And where I go, you come with me." 130
　"Ah, no, my love, no longer so.
I'll tell you why; then I must go.
As I lay in the field this morning,
Beside the orchard, without warning,
I saw a company of knights,
Fitly armed, a noble sight.
They bid me come without delay
To meet their king that very day.
I answered boldly, somewhat hot,
I owed them nothing and would not. 140
　"They rode away as if aghast,
And then their king drew up as fast,
With a hundred knights and more
And damsels also, several score,
All on steeds of snowy white
And dressed in white clothes, pure and bright.
I never saw before, I swear,
So fine a grouping anywhere.
That king must govern wealth untold.
Not silver was his crown, nor gold, 150
But shaped from one great precious stone;

And like the beaming sun it shone.
   "I tell you I had hardly wakened
When willy-nilly I was taken
And made to rouse myself and ride
Upon a palfrey by his side.
He brought me to his palace then,
Adorned beyond the dreams of men,
And showed me castles, meadows, towers,
Rivers, forests, fields of flowers,   160
The riches of his wide domain;
And then he brought me back again
To where he'd found me, near the trees,
And said as one to be appeased:
   " 'Tomorrow, lady, you must be
Beneath this selfsame grafted tree.
We'll come for you and you must go
To live among us evermore,
And if you make the least delay
We'll find and snatch you clean away.   170
We'll rip your tender limbs apart.
You can't escape by any art,
For even torn in pieces so
We'll bear you with us when we go.' "
   When Orfeo found out what had passed,
"My heart!" he cried. "My love, alas!
I'd far prefer to lose my life
Than lose you thus, my queen and wife!"
   He asked his men what he should do,
But they said nothing. No one knew.   180
The next day dawning fine and clear,
He armed himself in all his gear,
And marshaled up his thousand knights,
Each one steeled by many fights,
And then the anguished queen and he
Went out to wait beneath the tree.
The knights formed shield-walls on each side.
They'd never stir a step, they cried.
They'd die in place that very day

Before their queen was borne away.   190
    But yet for all those men and arms,
The fairies fetched the queen by charms.
Their spell took hold; she wasn't there.
She'd gone away; no man knew where!
Then there was wailing and great woe!
The king went to his chamber so
And threw himself upon the floor
With doleful cries and grief so sore
His earthly life was nearly ended;
His loss could never be amended.   200
    He called his barons all the same,
Knights and earls well known to fame.
When all he summoned were at hand,
"My men," he said, "hear my command.
I name my steward, whom you know,
To be your master. I must go.
He shall rule here in my stead
And keep my lands and minions fed.
Alas, I've lost my darling queen,
The fairest lady ever seen.   210
I'll brook no other, I protest.
No, I'll take to the wilderness,
And live at large forevermore
Where winter raves and wild beasts roar.
If you should learn that I am dead,
Call a council, on my head,
And choose yourselves another king.
Do as you will with all my things."
    Then there was weeping in the hall
And grating cries among them all.   220
No one could be clearly heard,
For wailing drowned out every word!
The knights knelt down before the man
And begged him to rescind his plan
And not abandon them to woe.
"I won't," he said. "I'm bound to go."
    All his kingdom he forsook;

A pilgrim's robe was all he took.
He had no kirtle, no, nor hood,
Shirt or belt or other goods.   230
He kept his harp, though—that was fate—
And bore it barefoot out the gate.
He wouldn't take his fondest men.
O there was woeful weeping then,
When he who once had worn the crown
Went like a pauper from the town!
    Through wild lands, sirs, for many a day
And many a night he made his way.
No one came to give him aid;
He saw his health and comfort fade.   240
He who'd gone in regal fur
And slept in state, now like a cur
Curled up in spite of frost and storm
With only leaves to keep him warm.
He'd once owned castles, farms, and towers,
Rivers, woodlands, walks, and flowers;
But now in snow and numbing frost,
He made his bed on frozen moss.
He'd once had noble knights at hand
And ladies, too, at his command;   250
Now naught was orderly or neat;
Wild serpents slithered round his feet.
He who'd had his choice of foods,
Meat and drink and other goods,
Must claw and dig like any brute
To feed himself on paltry roots.
    In summer, sirs, he gathered fruit
And meager berries on his route.
In winter when the days were dark
He lived on grass and roots and bark.   260
His body shriveled; he was hounded
By wounds and illnesses compounded.
Lord! Who could ever tell his tears
Or how he suffered full ten years?
His black beard, like a beastly pelt,

Reached thick and tangled to his belt.
    The harp, his one remaining pleasure,
He'd hidden well, his only treasure.
But when the air was clear and bright
He'd take it out, as well he might,   270
And harp on it with all his will.
Through all the woods the sound would trill.
He charmed the beasts; in companies
They'd come to gather at his knees,
And all the wild birds, shy and free,
Would settle in the nearest tree
To hear the harp sing in his hands.
His harping held them as with bands.
But when he paused or stopped his play,
The beasts roused up and ran away.   280
    He sometimes saw, if he was wary,
His rival lord, the King of Fairy,
Come forth to hunt there with his rout
And ride the country all about
With far, dim cries and distant blowing
And pallid hounds and faint helloing.
They took no beasts, not deer nor fawn,
Nor could he follow when they'd gone.
At other times the man might see
A host ride by him bold and free,   290
At least a thousand armored knights,
Each fitted out for mortal fights.
The men seemed good ones, fierce and stout;
They rode to battle, banners out,
Each warrior with his sword in hand,
But then they'd vanish from the land.
    And then at times he saw by chance
Lords and ladies at the dance—
All elegance and courtly graces,
With lively steps and stately paces.   300
Drums and trumpets kept the beat,
Fine minstrelsy for dancing feet.
One day he saw along his way

Sixty ladies, bright and gay,
Sweet and gentle, every one,
And not a man to spoil their fun.
Each bore a falcon on her hand
To hunt a stretch of bottomland.
They found good game in that low haunt:
Mallards, herons, cormorants.   310
As fowl rose squawking from the water,
The falcons marked each one for slaughter.
Each hawk stooped down and killed its prey,
And Orfeo laughed at their display.
    "My faith," he said, "a pretty game.
By God, I'll join them in the same.
I once was glad to see such play."
He rose and started off that way.
He hastened to a lady's side
And, lo! It couldn't be denied—   320
Riding there before his eyes
Was his dear queen, Dame Heurodis!
They watched each other, deeply stirred,
But neither one could speak a word.
She saw his dirt and wretchedness,
Who once was coddled to excess,
And wept bright tears from either eye.
The ladies noticed, standing by,
And bore her off without delay.
She had no choice. She might not stay.   330
    "Alack," he cried, "this feeds my woe.
Why don't I die? I'll never know.
What a wretch! It can't be right
To live in spite of such a sight.
Alas, I'm weary of my life:
Not one word to greet my wife!
And she said nothing! Which is worse?
Ach, why should not my hard heart burst?
In faith," he said then, "come what may
Where those fair ladies ride today,   340
That's where I'll go, upon my breath!

I'll follow, be it life or death!"
He snatched his robe to take their track.
Hanging his harp across his back,
He squared his shoulders, set his chin,
Resolved to go through thick or thin.
The ladies rode into a rock;
He followed close and felt no shock.
Through the stone for quite three miles
They made their way by hidden aisles 350
To a land not far away,
As sunny as a summer day.
Plains stretched before him, smooth and green,
No hills or valleys to be seen.
A castle rose above the mead;
None ever matched its wealth, indeed.
The outer wall of its great mass
Was made of shining crystal glass.
   A hundred towers stood round about
With crenellated guard posts stout. 360
Gold buttresses arched up to float
Above deep footings in the moat.
Each piece of vaulting was picked out
By bright enamel tiles and grout.
Inside were many spacious halls
Where jewels paved the floors and walls.
Its meanest pillar, I've been told,
Was solid, brilliant, burnished gold.
That land never lost its light,
For when it should be dark at night, 370
The jewels that everywhere were strewn
Flamed out like shining suns at noon.
No one could count or hold in mind
Its precious work of every kind.
Each thing that met Sir Orfeo's eyes
Proclaimed he was in Paradise.
   The ladies alighted, went inside.
He followed, not to be denied,
But had to knock upon the gate.

The porter came and asked him straight: 380
"Tell me, man, what brought you here?"
     "I've been a minstrel many years.
I'll entertain your lord today
And bring him comfort, if I may."
     The portal opened wide to show
A brilliant courtyard, all aglow;
But then he saw there, all around,
A sorry party on the grounds.
Humans whom the fairies caught—
Men thought them dead, but they were not.   390
Some stood up without a head;
Some had no arms, but stumps instead.
Some had gaping wounds full sad,
And some were tied up, raving mad.
Some on horses, there by fate,
And some who'd strangled as they ate.
Some were dripping. They had drowned.
Some blackened hulks the fire had found.
Wives lay groaning, great with child—
Some seeming dead, some driven wild.   400
Many more lay there besides
Just as they had lived and died.
Each was from our own world taken,
By fairies sought, by men forsaken.
     There Orfeo saw his own dear wife,
Dame Heurodis, who'd been his life.
She seemed to sleep beneath her tree.
Her clothing told him it was she.
He watched these people, held in thrall,
Then went inside the central hall.   410
Ah, there he met a seemly sight;
A canopy stood tall and bright,
And underneath it sat the king
And his fair lady, fresh as spring.
Their crowns and clothing blazed with light.
His eyes were dazzled by the sight.
     Orfeo blinked and looked around,

Approached the king and, kneeling down,
He said, "O lord, if you agree,
Be pleased to hear my minstrelsy."   420
    The king demanded, "Who are you?
And, pray, what are you here to do?
Not I nor any fairy peer
Sent for you or asked you here.
I tell you, since my reign began
There's never been another man
So foolish he would come to us,
Except he had been summoned first."
    "Sire," said Orfeo, "as you can tell,
I'm just a man with songs to sell.   430
And hungry minstrels, I'm afraid,
Must seek out lords, for that's our trade.
We are often turned away,
But we at least must try to play."
    Before the king he sat him down.
His harp strings rang, a merry sound.
He tuned the ones that went amiss,
And raised a shower of notes—what bliss!
Each fairy in the place that day
Came to the hall to hear him play.   440
They sat themselves around his feet,
And, oh, his melodies were sweet!
The king attended, sitting still,
Listening with all his will.
He took great joy in Orfeo's art.
The queen did too; he touched her heart.
    The sovereign power of Orfeo's songs
Convinced the king he'd judged him wrong.
"Minstrel," he said, when all grew still,
"Ask for payment what you will.   450
Your music's worth a rich reward;
Speak, and you'll see my regard."
    "Sir," he answered, "let me pray
That you will give me, now, today,
That same fine lady, bright and free,

Who sleeps beneath the grafted tree."
    "No," said the king, "for heaven's sake.
A sorry couple you would make.
For you are black and rough and lean,
And she is fair, a proper queen!   460
A loathly mismatch, as you see,
To place her in your company."
    "Yet," said Orfeo, "gentle king,
It would be a fouler thing
To hear a falsehood come from you.
You said just now—you know it's true—
You'd give me anything. All heard.
Come, my lord, now keep your word."
    "Alas," said the king, "it must be so.
Then take her by the hand and go,   470
And I must wish you joy of her."
    Orfeo knelt and thanked him there.
He took his wife up by the hand
And led her quickly from that land.
They left the country, all and some,
Along the paths by which they'd come.
Outside the rock they traveled on
And came to Winchester anon,
Back to his home, his city free,
But no one guessed that it was he.   480
For fear they'd know his looks or sound
He stopped a bit outside of town,
And with a beggar by the way
He took a lodging, far from gay,
For himself and his dear wife
(He seemed a man of humble life),
And asked for tidings of the town.
Who ruled the kingdom all around?
    The beggar landlord searched his wit
And told the story, every bit: 490
How their queen was snatched away
By fairy magic one spring day,
And how their king had spent ten years

Among the wilds, for all their tears,
And how the steward ruled the land,
And more at Orfeo's command.
    Next day when it was almost noon
He left his lady in their room,
And dressed him in the beggar's clothes.
Now free to wander where he chose,   500
He took his harp into the town
So men could see him on the ground.
Knights and earls and ladies fair,
Barons and burghers, met him there.
"Ugh!" they said. "Ha! What a show!
Whose hair has ever drooped so low?
His beard hangs down below his knees!
His skin might be the bark of trees!"
    Then Orfeo chanced as he had planned
To come upon his former man   510
And cried aloud: "For charity,
Sir Steward, spare a word for me—
A harper come from heathen lands.
Favor me with your commands."
    The steward said, "Now come, man, come.
Of what I have, you shall have some.
I welcome every harper so
For my lost lord, Sir Orfeo."
Soon they were at the steward's table
With many others, weak or able.   520
Amid those trumpeters and drummers,
Harpers, fiddlers, and mummers,
Tunes rose up to fill the air
As Orfeo listened from his chair.
And then, my lords, when it grew still
He showed them all his matchless skill.
He struck the strings and harped them then
Songs never heard by other men.
Every man approved his art.
The steward looked up with a start   530
And saw the harp was Orfeo's.

"There is a tale, as I suppose,
In how you got that harp," he said.
"Perhaps you'll tell it now you're fed."
    "Lord," said Orfeo, "in a distant land,
Alone, and far from any man,
I found as fate or heaven willed
A man a lion pride had killed,
And wolves had worried, fierce and sharp.
Beside his body lay this harp.   540
And that was quite ten years ago."
    "Ah," said the steward, "woe on woe!
That was my lord, Sir Orfeo.
No other news could wound me so.
Now he is dead and I'm forlorn.
Alas, that I was ever born.
How will I ever bear this weight?
What marked him out for such a fate?"
    He fell at once into a swoon.
His barons clustered round, but soon   550
The man, though suffering, caught his breath.
There is no remedy for death.
King Orfeo knew well by then
His steward was loyal, still his man;
The fellow loved him as he ought.
And so he spoke, as if in thought:
"Steward, tell me, by your sword,
If I were Orfeo, your lord,
And I had suffered, cold and poor,
A wild man's life, and what is more,   560
Had dared to leave this world to bring
My wife back from the Fairy King,
And fetched her from the fairy mound
Homeward to the edge of town,
And lodged her in a beggar's home,
And then if I myself had come
To you, impoverished and unknown,
To see if you were still my own,
And if I found you good and true,

How could I rightly honor you?   570
Sir, let me tell you straightaway
You shall be king beyond my day.
If you'd rejoiced that I was dead,
You'd now be banned from here instead."
   Soon every man there in the hall
Knew the king, but most of all
The steward reveled in his lord.
He overthrew the dining board
And cast himself at Orfeo's feet.
Every man rose from his seat,   580
And called to make the rafters ring:
"Hail to Orfeo, our king!"
They all rejoiced, the faithful men,
And took him to his chamber then,
And bathed his limbs and shaved his beard.
His kingly looks soon reappeared.
   A great procession wound away
To bring the good queen home to stay,
With every sort of minstrelsy.
Lord! How they made melody!   590
All wept as, wonderstruck, they learned
Their king and queen had been returned.
Sir Orfeo wore his crown once more.
His wife was queen just as before.
They lived a long while afterward,
And then the steward reigned, I've heard.
   Breton harpers after them
Heard this marvel told by men,
Composed the lay you've heard, and, lo,
They named it after Orfeo: 600
"Sir Orfeo," a song of note
To sweeten any singer's throat.
Thus Orfeo outlived his care.
May God defend us everywhere!

ATHELSTON

A rough-and-ready example of popular Middle English romance, Athelston *appears in an early fifteenth-century manuscript with other vigorous tales such as* Sir Ysumbras *and* Bevis of Hampton. *No one else tells this story of Athelston, a tenth-century Saxon king involved in the Battle of Brunanburh. The tale is concocted of common themes—trials, false friends, last-minute reversals—braided into a completely unhistorical fantasy. However, the story rattles along at an entertaining clip, Athelston and Bishop Alric make rousing speeches, the two women have good parts, the villain is suitably slimy, and for all we know the beleaguered messenger may be galloping still.*

Athelston *is written in tail rhyme, an unpretentious form Chaucer satirizes through the story of Sir Thopas in* The Canterbury Tales. *In tail rhyme, eight-syllable couplets are followed by shorter lines that rhyme with each other throughout a stanza, here an irregular unit ranging from six to twelve lines.*

The made-up nature of the story and its inclusion in a manuscript with a number of moral tales and saints' lives could indicate the author had a special point to make—or several of them. Sir Wymond, motivated by an Iago-like envy, shows the danger of kings being misled by false counsel. Athelston is irascible and rash. The writer was probably also concerned about the balance of powers between the king, Parliament, and church. His romance would certainly have reminded hearers of the twelfth-century conflict between Thomas à Becket and Henry II. It could be dangerous to address such matters directly, so setting his story in a distant and largely imaginary past might have been a prudent decision on the writer's part.

Lord of power, God of hosts,
Father, Son, and Holy Ghost,
   Deliver us from sin.
Lord, lend us grace upon this sod
To love our holy church and God
   So we may heaven win.
Now listen to me, sirs, attend.
My story shows how falseness ends

For those who live therein.
Of four confederates I tell,   10
Who here in England once did dwell,
   Brothers, though not kin.

Each man was a messenger,
With English letters in his purse,
   As it was told to me.
By a forest all four met
Close to where a cross was set,
   Beneath a linden tree.
As my story tells, each man
Came here from a different land,   20
   For they had crossed the sea.
And yet, for love, on meeting here
Each joined in brotherhood to swear
   He'd serve the other three.

Now, of these four, the oldest one
Was a knight called Athelston,
   The king's own cousin dear.
He was of the king's true line—
His uncle's son, by God's design—
   No other kin was nearer.   30
Now at length, well and fair,
The old king died, without an heir,
   What's more, without a peer.
So Athelston, the uncle's son,
Put forth his claim, and when he won
   Was crowned with gold most clear.

As free a king as any other,
He sent at once for his sworn brothers
   And gave them their reward.
The first became the Earl of Dover.   40
This poor man rose to lord it over
   The castle and its hoard.
The next he made the Earl of Stone.

Sir Egelond, as he was known,
   Became a famous lord.
The king gave Egelond to wife
His own dear sister, Dame Edyff,
   To join him at his board.

The fourth sworn brother was a clerk
Well grounded in God's holy work.   50
   Alric was his name.
As Canterbury[1] was vacant then
And subject to the new king's hand,
   This Alric got the same.
And he deserved his bishop's crook,[2]
For he could read in any book,
   A good priest free of blame.
The king thus served his brothers well,
And earned himself, as it befell,
   Great riches and wide fame.   60

Sir Egelond, the Earl of Stone,
Upheld the kingdom and the throne,
   A true man as you'll hear.
God approved his nobleness,
For his Lady soon was blessed
   With two boy children dear.
One was fifteen winters old,
The other thirteen, I was told,
   And neither knew a peer.
Both were white as lily flowers,   70
Red as roses in their bowers,
   And bright as blossoms clear.

The king as he loved his own life,
Prized Sir Egelond and his wife

---

1. All three seats—Dover, Canterbury, and Stone (or Stane)—are between London and the English Channel; Stone is about seventeen miles outside of London.

2. A bishop's symbol of pastoral authority.

And both their handsome sons.
He loved their family over all.
In private or within his hall,
　　Their counsel often won.
The Earl of Dover chafed at this
(His name was Wymond, by my bliss),   80
　　But answer had he none.
He aped a true man in his guise,
To better spread malicious lies
　　And see his foes undone.

Now this Sir Wymond slyly thought:
"Their love, I swear, will come to naught
　　If my words still can sting."
He bid his servants to prepare,
For off to London he would fare
　　To counsel with the king.   90
When Wymond came into the court
The king called out in friendly sort,
　　"Sir, say what news you bring."
The earl stood silent, stern, and glum.
He let the king ask how he'd come,
　　How fast, and suchlike things.

"Say, did you come by Canterbury
Where the priests sing out so merry,
　　Both early and full late?
How did you find that noble clerk,   100
The bishop, known for holy work?
　　Pray, tell me of his state.
And came you by the Earl of Stone,
My loved retainer in his home?
　　Say, did you pass his gate?
What can you tell me of that knight
And both his young sons, bold and bright,
　　Or Edyff, his dear mate?"

"Sir," said Wymond, "I must say,
By Canterbury my road lay.   110

I saw your bishop there.
He blesses you, the noble clerk
Who knows so much of God's true work,
    A priest without compare!
I later rode by Stone as well
And spoke to Egelond as it fell,
    And with the countess rare.
They fare full well, my lord, in truth,
As do their sons, the noble youths."
    This pleased the king, I swear. 120

"Sir King," said Wymond, "if I may,
Let's to your chamber make our way;
    My counsel you shall hear.
And there I'll tell you something sweet.
A gladder word you'll never meet,
    In all this hundred year."
The king agreed. He couldn't know
This villain would abuse him so,
    And went forth with good cheer.
Yet once within his private room 130
Sir Wymond spread his lies to doom
    His onetime brother dear.

"Sir King," the wicked plotter said,
"I hope I never see you dead,
    As long as I have life.
For by Him who this world won,
I owe you everything I've done:
    Your help has let me thrive.
But there's a traitor in your land.
He'll spoil your honor if he can 140
    By slander or by knife.
Back-biting is the least he'll do.
I fear he means to murder you,
    By Christ's dear wounds, all five!"

Then said the king, "Tell me aright,
Sir, do I know this man by sight?

Say, what is his fame?"
"No!" said the traitor. "I will not,
For all that gold has ever bought,
    Or I'd be put to shame . . .   150
Unless, my king, you give your word
That you'll tell no one where you heard
    The name that I shall name."
My lords, the king raised up his hand,
And swore his faith to that false man.
    The Devil take the same!

"Sir King," he said, "you made me knight.
And now you've pledged within my sight,
    My part in this to hide.
Certainly it is no other   160
But Egelond, your own sworn brother,
    Who'd slay you out of pride.
He's made your sister understand
He should be king of all your land.
    He's won her to his side.
He'll give you poison, lord—he's sly—
Then seize the kingdom when you die,
    By Jesus Christ, our guide."

The king swore, "By God's holy feet,
I shall taste neither drink nor meat   170
    Until the man is caught!
Moreover, both his sons and wife
Must fall with him and taste the knife.
    They're privy to this plot!"
"Sir," said the traitor in reply,
"I would not see my brother die . . .
    But follow your own thought."
His end attained, he turned about,
Rode back to his own strong redoubt—
    God bring his lies to naught!   180

His scheme began to work that day.
A man was sought without delay

To parley for his lord.
They brought the king a hearty man
Whose name was also Athelston,
   A foundling, as I've heard.
Stout letters, issued from the throne,
This fellow bore at once to Stone—
   They wouldn't be deferred.
They called the earl upon his life   190
To bring his two sons and his wife,
   Upon the king's own word.

What's more, the letters plainly told
The king required the sons full bold
   To make each one a knight.
Each letter bore the royal seal
To show the messages were real.
   His man rode out of sight.

The messenger, a noble one,
Spurred his horse into a run.   200
   He did not spare his steed.
He found the earl as he had planned
And put the letters in his hand,
   Knelt down and bid him read.
"Sir," he said to play his part,
"My news should stir a noble's heart.
   I pray you, sir, take heed.
Because he loves the countess, lo,
The king will knight your sons. And so
   To London you must speed.   210

"Our king, who holds the countess dear,
Will knight your sons to give her cheer—
   And serve your honor too.
Your lady wife should be on hand,
In keeping with the king's command,
   To see all he will do."
Then earl protested though beguiled:
"My wife is heavy, great with child,

And as it seems to me,
She mustn't leave her folks or room   220
For anyone, so swells her womb,
   Till she delivered be."

They went to where the countess lay,
Read her the letters, I heard say,
   And told her all the news.
The countess said, "Sirs, as I'm blessed,
I'll not hold back an hour or rest;
   The king can't be refused.

"To see my sons made knights so soon . . .
I'll be at court tomorrow noon;   230
   I cannot linger here.
As Christ inspired the king, my lord,
To grant them knighthood with his sword,
   I'll be there, never fear!"
The earl bid all his men prepare;
His family would to London fare
   With servants and their gear.
Westminster was the king's chief home,
And there they met with Athelston,
   Whose summons brought them there.   240

                                      •

Sirs, on the spot the earl was seized
And roughly bound upon his knees,
   And with him both his sons.
Loudly did the countess cry,
"Mercy, brother, or I die!
   Say why are we undone?
How, lord, have we offended you,
To make you treat us as you do?
   This plot is lately spun!"
The king was almost mad by then;   250
"Take her hence," he told his men,
   And looked about him, stunned.

A squire who loved the stricken countess
Approached the queen at her behest
   And told her what you've heard.
Garlands of cherries by her lay.
She cast them down and made her way
   To the hall, where all this stirred.
"Sir King, I have before you come—
Great with child, your girl or son—   260
   Lord, listen to my word:
This earl and countess grant to me
Until tomorrow. Set them free
   From where they lie immured.

"Then charge them, lord, with my consent
Before your lords in Parliament."
"Dame," said the king, "now get away!
I won't relent for all you say.
   No, you must understand:
By Him who wears the Crown of Thorns,   270
They all shall hang tomorrow morn,
   If I still rule this land!"

Listening, the queen grew sick
As if he'd struck her with a stick.
   Her tears began to fall.
As surely as I tell this tale,
She knelt down on the floor, all pale,
   Still pleading for them all.
"By God," the king said, "they shall die,
And yet you thwart my will, or try.   280
   I'll pay you in this hall!"
And as he spoke, the king grew wild
And kicked her side and slew their child.
   She fainted by the wall.

Ladies ran to tend the queen
And help her from the shameful scene,
   And they had much to do.

For there within a little space
She bore a boy-child in that place,
   As bright as blossoms new. 290
His hue was lovely, white and red,
But, sirs, alas, the boy was dead,
   Crushed by his father's shoe!
Thus tyrants will do what they please
And rage and kill and smite and seize—
   But this one suffered too!

Next, the queen, as you shall hear
Summoned her own messenger.
   She didn't keep him long.
She bid him wend to Canterbury 300
Where the clerks sing loud and merry
   At Mass and Evensong.
"This letter to the bishop take,
And pray him for Our Dear Lord's sake
   To right this shameful wrong.
He loves the earl, as I have seen,
More than me, though I am queen,
   And, sir, his arm is strong.

"I have a great estate in Spain.
That earldom, sir, you may attain, 310
   If you will use your might.
A hundred coins shall be your fee,
Just bring the bishop from his see.
   God aid you in your flight!"
"My lady, keep your property.
It's yours," he said, "not meant for me.
   Thereto I have no right.
But for your love and golden fee
I'll do your bidding as you see.
   I'll speak to him tonight. 320

"I've ridden thirty miles a day,
Madam, on the hardest way,

And no one saw me shrink.
But add another twenty-five!
That's hard indeed, so may I thrive,
    As anyone might think.
And now we're near the end of prime   *about 10 a.m.*
And yet I've had no chance to dine,
    Or ale or wine to drink.
Let me eat, and then I'll fare—   330
May Jesus keep them in His care—
    Before I sleep a wink.

The good man ate and went his way.
Spurring fast to earn his pay,
    He rode by Charing Cross.
He cantered next along the Fleet,
Then clattered down the nearest street
    Upon a noble horse.
He parted folks on either hand
Where London Bridge the river spanned.   340
    His journey brought no loss.
And then past Stone to Sittingbourne
He kept his way without a turn,
    Spared not for mire or moss.

Next, onward, straight as any bee,
Past Ospring on the way to Blee.   *places on the road to Canterbury*
    From there he saw the town.
To Canterbury then, at length,
There where the bishop sat in strength,
    A lord of great renown.   350
Sirs, he heard the morning bell
Ring in London, I heard tell,
    At the start of all his trials,
Yet rode to Canterbury then
To hear the Evensong begin—   *around 6 or 7 p.m.*
    Well more than fifty miles!

The messenger refused to wait.
He rode within the palace gate,

And found the bishop in.
They gave him hearty welcome there,   360
For they all held the queen full dear
   With all her noble kin.
The man drew out his lady's note.
He showed the bishop what she wrote,
   And bid him read therein.
Before the letter was half read
The bishop cried aloud with dread
   And tears ran to his chin.

The bishop called then for a horse
And set his men upon their course.   370
   "Bid them," he said, "now fare.
Let them ride ahead, I say,
Alert my manors on the way—
   Ride hard and never spare.
Arrange it so that each five miles
I find a fresh horse—no denials—
   Well shod and saddled there,
For happy I will never be
Until I may my brother see
   And free him from this care."   380

On nine fresh mounts the bishop rode
Until dawn broke and morning showed,
   In romance as we read.
But certainly, as I may tell,
On London Bridge the queen's man fell.
   The ride had killed his steed.
"Alas," he said, "that I was born.
My horse is dead, and I'm forlorn.
   He answered every need.
Yesterday, upon the ground,   390
He was worth a hundred pounds,
   A princely horse, indeed!"

"Let be!" said the bishop with a nod,
Our holy father under God,

And told the messenger:
"Leave this mourning for your steed
And think instead on our great need,
 The grief that brought us here.
For if I may my brother save—
Preserve him from an early grave—   400
 Then you may make glad cheer.
The rich reward that I shall give,
Will see you through if you should live
 To see your hundredth year!"

The bishop, sirs, would not abide
But mounted up again to ride
 Till Westminster was in sight.
The messenger came on foot as well
But no one else, the story tells,
 Not servant, squire, or knight.   410
That selfsame day the king arose
And walked down to the Minster close,
 A man of ample might.
With him went both priest and clerk,
Ministers of holy work,
 To pray God for the right.

When he to the church was come
Before the cross he knelt with some,
 Beseeching God full well:
"Now, Jesus in the Trinity,   420
I pray you, grant a boon to me,
 As you once harrowed hell.
If any innocents may lie
Within my prisons, far or nigh,
 Complaining in their cells,
Lord, if they're guiltless, hear my plea:
Don't let them languish; set them free.
 Don't leave them there to dwell."

Now having told his heart's desire,
The king looked back into the choir   430

And saw the bishop there.
Surprised to see the good man's face,
He went to greet him in his place
   And spoke to him full fair:
"Greetings, brother, welcome here.
As you're God's priest, we hold you dear."
   The man replied, "Take care!
My precious brother, may you speed,
I never had so great a need
   Since I was born, I swear.   440

"My faithful brother, now take heed.
Do not condemn your friends to bleed
   Unless it must be so.
By Him who wears the Crown of Thorn
Release them till tomorrow morn.
   By then, lord, we may know—
And all agree by one consent,
Lord, in your open Parliament—
   That they have earned this blow.
If you won't do this, as I say,   450
We'll both regret this sorry day,
   For God will send us woe."

At that, the king turned red as fire.
No one has seen a wrath more dire
   Than his now grew to be.
He took his oath by sun and moon:
"They shall be drawn and hanged by noon—
   As you, my lord, shall see!
Lay down your cross, you wretched knave!
Your miter and that ring I gave!   460
   Be wise, my lord, and flee.
Now get you quickly from my sight,
Or I will take your life by right.
   Your death will be my fee!"

But then the bishop in the church,
Who knew so well God's holy work,

Spoke boldly to the king:
"I know, Sir King, betimes you gave
Me my cross and bishop's stave,
    My miter and my ring.   470
My bishopric you gave me, true—
But I'll take Christendom from you!
    No priest shall pray or sing.
Neither maiden child nor knave
Shall be baptized against the grave.
    My lord, your heart will sting!

"I shall cry through every town
So people tear their churches down
    And fill the ruins with thorn.
And you shall lie out cold and sick,   480
A god-forsaken heretic.
    You'll grieve that you were born!

"Though you should die and I might see,
You'll never be absolved by me,
    Your soul trapped in death's cave.
And I shall range through every land
To rally strong men to my hand,
    My brother's life to save.
I shall call down on your head
Drought and famine. Till you're dead,   490
    That's all that you shall have.
I won't leave a bit of earth
Worth the buckle on your girth;
    You'll envy any slave!"

The bishop went out by the door,
And found his men and many more
    Were waiting in the yard.
He led this band into a street
Where worthy lords of England meet,
    Each riding with his guard.   500
On their knees the nobles kneeled,
Besought his blessing, and appealed.

He gave them no regard.
They saw he had no cross or ring,
For those were taken by the king.
    By God, his heart was charred!

A knight spoke with a mild, soft voice,
"Where is your ring? Where is your cross?
    Sir, tell us if you will."
He said, "My lords, your cursed king   510
Has seized my cross and other things.
    My faith, he used me ill!
And so I have condemned your land,
No English priest, by my command,
    Shall sing or christen till
The king grants me my brother knight,
His wife and children, fair and bright,
    Whom now he vows to kill."

The knight said, "Bishop, turn again;
We'll follow you and end his reign.   520
    Your brother shall be served.
Unless the king grants you this boon,
His own head shall be forfeit soon.
    He'll have what he's deserved.
We'll throw down all his halls and bowers,
Every castle, all his towers;
    Not one shall be preserved.
Though he's our king and wears the crown,
We'll shake him off and cast him down.
    Christ's laws shall be observed."   530

But as they spoke of suchlike things,
Here came two knights sent by the king,
    And said, "Good lord, abide.
Take back your ring; have back your cross.
Relent, good sir. You'll feel no loss.
    The king repents his pride.
He freely grants the earl to you,

His noble wife and children too,
   So you stay by his side.
Retract, my lord, what you resolved;   540
Grant the king may be absolved—
   And England, far and wide."

The king came next along the way.
He freed the earl that very day,
   And to the bishop said:
"This earl, his sons, my sister too—
All these now owe their lives to you.
   Without you they'd be dead."
Then said the bishop in reply,
"My king, we'll test them by and by.   550
   We'll sound them, never dread.
If they are guilty, one or all,
They'll say as much within your hall,
   Not risk my trial instead."

Then at the holy man's desire
Retainers stoked a mighty fire,
   As romancers recall.
They heaped the wood around their wares—
A pathway formed of nine plowshares,
   A walkway to appall.   560
Up spoke the king, "What does this mean?"
"Sire," said the bishop, "if they're clean,
   They'll show it to us all."
Then said the king, this Athelston,
"This trial would daunt anyone,
   Whatever may befall."

The men fetched forth Sir Egelond—
No truer earl was ever found—
   Before the fire so bright.
Pulled off his shoes, as I suppose,   570
And took away his scarlet hose,
   Gear suited for a knight.

Nine times the bishop blessed those shares
The earl must tread with earnest prayers
   To show his cause was right.
The knight went scatheless, foot or hand,
Before the high lords of the land,
   And thanked God in His might.

They led him forth with humble cheer;
At Saint Paul's altar he appeared,   580
   A holy place of power.
Down upon his knees he fell
And thanked the Lord who harrowed hell,
   And Mary in that hour.

The bishop then stood up to say,
"Now shall the children go the way
   That their good father did."
They took their shoes and scarlet hose,
Divested them of all their clothes;
   So nothing could be hid.   590
The shares were hotter, glowing red,
And both boys quaked with mortal dread.
   The bishop was their guide.
He gave them each a tender look
And said in tones that never shook:
   "Lads, let your fears subside."

With that the boys stood forth and laughed:
"Is this a fire? Why, don't be daft!"
   They walked their way apace.
They stayed unblemished, foot and hand,   600
Watched by the high lords of the land,
   And thanked God for His grace.

They went too with humble cheer
To Saint Paul's altar, cleansed of fear,
   To have their act proclaimed.
Once more the bishop stood to say,

"The wife must go the selfsame way,
   Sir King, lest she be blamed."

They led her out, the countess mild,
Just as she was, full great with child,   610
   In ancient tales we read.
And while she walked the path she must,
The bishop prayed with pious trust
   To Christ, whose wounds still bleed:
"God forbid a wicked soul
Should brave this fire and come out whole!"
   The noble wife agreed.

Then the countess said a prayer
And stepped upon the foremost share
   That burned there fair and bright.   620
She walked the first third of the way
Then paused a while to turn in play
   As if the trial were light.
But then her labor pains came strong,
Shook her back and cramped her womb,
   Before the watchers' sight.

When her pains decreased, men say,
She walked her course the nearest way,
   Though blood burst from her nose.[3]
That's all she suffered, foot or hand,   630
Before the lords of all the land—
   She thanked God, heaven knows.
They led her from the common hall,
Surrounded by her ladies all;
   These flocked around her close.
She knelt upon the pavement, faint,
And there was born her son, our saint,
   As blessed as a rose.

---

3. A similar burning-plowshare trial is associated with Queen Emma, mother of St. Edward the Confessor.

No other saint was born this way.
They brought them back without delay,   640
   The baby and his dame.
The humbled king and bishop free
Baptized the babe for all to see,
   And Edmund was his name.[4]
The king said, "Half my land I give
Unto this young lad while I live,
   With funds to keep the same,
And when I die, may heaven bring
That he serve England as her king.
   God save us all from blame!"   650

Then said the bishop to the king,
"Say, sire, who caused these evil things?
   Who stirred up all this ill?"
The king replied, "No, I'm not free.
Don't ask to hear his name from me,
   For I must keep it still.
Sir, I swore stoutly by Saint Anne
I never will betray the man
   Who bent me to his will.
These folk are saved by your device;   660
Leave the rest, lord, where it lies;
   Let be, for all your skill."

The bishop said, "Lord, from this hour,
You may rely upon my power:
   Sir, I'll absolve you clean.
You'll be as one who's just baptized.
Do, my lord, as I advise.
   Speak out and rest serene.
I swear to you on book and bell
If you will name this fiend from hell,   670
   I'll pay him for his spleen:

   4. This seems to refer to St. Edmund of East Anglia, a ninth-century king killed by
Vikings. His remains are at Bury St. Edmunds, not far from London.

He himself will go the way
Your good sworn brother went today.
   His falseness shall be seen!"

Then said the king, "For praise or blame,
I'll render up his wicked name,
   Not scruple and hold back.
Certainly, it is no other
Than Wymond, sir, our own sworn brother,
   And may his road be black!"   680
"By heaven," said the bishop then,
"I thought he was the truest man
   That trod this earthly track.
If the dastard's guilt is clear,
We'll draw and hang him, lord, I swear—
   His every bone shall crack!"

Now that he knew, without surmise,
Who had spread such evil lies,
   He told his messenger:
"Go to Dover, strong and fair.   690
Tell the earl that you find there—
   A traitor without peer—
That Egelond, whom he loved once,
Was drawn and hanged with both his sons.
   He'll listen, never fear.
His lady's captured, say, in chains.
She'll never venture out again
   Except upon her bier."

The messenger was quick to go.
He took his horse; he wasn't slow.   700
   To Dover he soon came.
In his hall he found the man,
Placed a letter in his hand,
   And then rehearsed the same:
"Sir Egelond and his sons are dead,
Drawn and hanged, upon my head;

His earldom you may claim.
The countess is bound up in chains.
She won nothing for her pains
    But infamy and shame."   710

The earl's cursed heart rose up on high,
He thanked God for his wicked lie:
    "It brought all this," he said.
"Fellow, you are lucky too.
Here are fine gold coins for you,
    Because my plans have sped."
The messenger then made a plea:
"Sir, let me have a horse in fee,
    One able and well bred.
For yesterday my good horse fell.   720
He ran your errand all too well,
    And now he's lying dead."

"My mounts are fat and too well fed.
Ride them? You might be thrown instead."
    The earl said to him then.
"If a horse of mine should slay you so,
The king would be cast down with woe
    To lose so good a man."

The man went out and bought a steed,
One to serve in every need.   730
    No better could be found.
Astride again, sirs, I attest,
The messenger refused to rest,
    But reined the horse around.
"Noble earl," he said, "good day.
Come to London when you may.
    Your master's love is sound."
Then with his spurs he struck the steed,
And rode to Gravesend at good speed,   *on the way back to London*
    Full forty miles of ground.   740

He waited for the traitor there,
Nor was it long. The earl appeared
   And they to London rode.
They came within the palace yard,
Then went inside, through all the guards
   By Athelston's abode.

The earl stepped forth to kiss his lord,
Who turned away with, "On my word!
   By God and by Saint John!
Through your villainy, I swear,   750
I killed—yes, I—my rightful heir.
   His life is now foregone!"

The earl shrank back and fast denied
That he'd misled the king or lied,
   Afraid before them all.
The bishop took him by the hand;
Without a word he led the man
   Into the king's wide hall.
The bishop held the false earl fast;
No priest there would absolve his past,   760
   Whatever might befall.
And then said good King Athelston,
"Let him do what his peers have done,
   To prove his truth withal."

When they heard their king's desire,
Retainers sprang to lay the fire,
   In romances as we read.
They banked it high, the truth to show,
By nine steel plowshares in a row,
   Fired red as any glede.   *ember*
Nine times the bishop blessed the way
The traitor had to walk that day
   To answer for his deed.
He walked indeed unto the third

But there he fell without a word—
  A liar, all agreed.

Egelond's children sprang forth then,
Raced to the fire to grasp the man
  And draw him from the flame.
They took their oath by book and bell: 780
"Before you die, lord, you shall tell
  What was your wicked aim."
"I see," he said, "upon my head,
I'm ruined and shall soon be dead;
  I answer you in shame.
I thought the good king's love was such:
To me too little, to him too much.
  Plain envy was to blame."

Knowing how he went astray,
Men brought five horses where he lay.   790
  The man was firmly tied.
They dragged him bare, no coat or helm,
Through every street to one great elm,
  And there they hanged him high.
The boldest man would never dare
Retrieve his body rotting there,
  Disgraced for his foul lie.
May Jesus Christ, our blessed friend,
Bring no false man a better end
  Than such a death to die!   800

SAINT ERKENWALD

This alliterative poem has sometimes been attributed to the author of Gawain
and the Green Knight, *but no matter who the writer was it is a fine piece of
work. Like Chaucer's "Prioress's Tale," which was written about the same time,
the story of London's seventh-century bishop Erkenwald is a miracle tale—and
a very clever one. A dead but uncorrupted pagan (we never learn the man's
name) is fortuitously baptized and released from Limbo when Saint Erken-
wald says the sacramental words just as his tears—here serving as baptismal
water—wet the dead man's face.*

*The poem is also remarkable for its historical awareness—the writer is well
versed in London's Roman and pagan past—and its interest as part of the Al-
literative Revival, a sudden resurgence in the north of England of nonmetri-
cal, nonrhyming alliterative verse. This harkening back to the Anglo-Saxon
poetic form may have been a provincial reaction against London's success and
swelling importance. In fact, commemorating one of London's forgotten saints
in alliterative verse may have been a subtle dig at the city for growing away
from its own origins.*

In London in England and not overlong[1]
After Christ was crucified to establish His church,
There was a bishop in that borough, sacred and blessed.
Saint Erkenwald, by my hope, was that holy man called.
In his time in that town the tallest of temples
Was thrown down entire to be turned to God's work,
For it had been heathen when Hengest ruled there,   *fifth-century Saxon king*
Who Saxons, unsought, had set on the kingdom.
He suppressed the best people, pursued them to Wales,
While the men who remained took up pagan beliefs.   10
Thus the realm endured renegade many rough years,
Till Saint Austin to Sandwich was sent by the pope[2]

1. The poet, a northerner from around Cheshire, regards England as almost a foreign
country.

2. St. Augustine of Canterbury, who was sent by Pope Gregory the Great in 597 as the
first missionary to England.

To preach to the people, replanting the truth,
And convert the community to Christ once again.
The saint toppled the temples that had turned to the Devil,
Cleansed them as churches reclaimed in Christ's name.
He excluded their idols, exchanged them for saints,
Named them anew, and enjoined them to mend.
Apollo's house once, was Saint Peter's now,
Mahomet's, Saint Margaret's, or Magdalene's church.   *St. Mary Magdalene*
The shrine of the sun was saved for Our Lady.
Jupiter, Juno, changed to Jesus or James
As Austin assoiled and assigned to our holy ones
Shrines sacred to Satan in Saxon times.

New Troy was their term for the town now named London.
Metropolis and master-town it remains to this day.
That city's chief church was consigned to a fiend—
The greatest of all their false gods, as I guess,
And solemnest of his sacrifices in Saxon lands.
The place and its premises were pledged to his name.   30
He owned three heathen temples throughout the Triapolises.   *London, York,*
In Britain's broad bounds they built only two more.   *and Chester*
Now of Saint Austin's see was this Erkenwald bishop,   *(England's chief cities)*
Living at London to lay down God's law.
He sat in the high seat of Saint Paul's cathedral—
Where once was the Triapolitan temple I told of—
While the old shrine was razed and reared up anew,
Reshaped by God's servants as a center for Christ.
Many a mason spent sweat to amend it,
Hewing hard stones with his well-tempered tools.   40
And as men grubbed in the ground there to gain a firm footing
To fix a fit bed to found fresh work upon,
Lo, their prying and probing produced a great prodigy,
Recorded in chronicles kept in those times.
For digging and delving down deep in the earth,
They encountered a platform supporting a tomb—
A trough of thick stone that was artfully trimmed,
Garnished with gargoyles shaped in gray marble.
The top of the tomb, enclosing its treasures,
Was marble itself and full masterfully made,   50
With a border embellished with bright golden letters,

But the symbols seemed strange where they stood in their rows.
Full fine were the figures, as all men there found them,
But no one could name one or knew what it meant.
Though broad-headed clerics blessed with good brains
Scanned the inscriptions, their meanings escaped them.
Now when news of this wonder-tomb noised through the town,
Men hurried by hundreds to see it themselves.
The citizens clustered there, constables, merchants,
And well-grounded masters proficient in trades.   60
Lads left their labors, went leaping abroad,
Romping and running in rioting rabbles.
Crowds of all kinds came in such crushing numbers,
In a short space it seemed the whole world swarmed the ground.
Then the mayor and his minions met near the marvel
And besought the sacristan securing the site   *church official*
To unlock the tomb lid and lay it aside,
For that congress would see what the casket enclosed.
At once, willing workers went at the job,
Putting pry bars in place and pinching them under,   70
Catching the corners with crowbars of iron.
Though the lid was right large, they soon laid it by.
And then marvels emerged to make all stand amazed,
Dazzled and dazed by the delights they discovered.
The gaping chest gleamed with a gay show of gold,
And a blissful, fresh body that lay at the bottom
Richly arrayed in the most regal robes.
A fine inner gown glistened gold on the man,
While precious large pearls palely shone from his shirt.
His great gilded sash gleamed with gold where it fastened   80
On a kingly fine cloak trimmed out in rich ermine—
Comely cloth covered with costly embroidery,
With a cloth-of-gold cap and a right royal crown.
A seemly gold scepter was set in his hand.
The man's clothes were all clean and had somehow kept free
Of dark mold or dirt or the damage of moths—
As bright and as brilliant in bold shining hues
As if they'd been buried just one day before.
His face was as fresh. Where the flesh was exposed
At his hands and his ears it appeared full of health.   90

Full rosy his cheeks were and ruddy his lips,
As if seconds before he had slipped into sleep.
It was idle for men then to ask one another
Whose body this was that was buried among them,
Or how long he had lain there with looks hardly changed.
Yet they lingered nearby to learn the lord's name.
"For sure," they asserted, "he should be remembered
As a king of our kind. His clothing shows that,
With the cut of his coffin. We cannot conceive
Men no longer know who this lord was in life."   100
Still, their care came to naught, for none could remember
By title or token the tale of the man.
No knowledge of elders, no note in their books,
Glossed that lord's life or his lore or his name.
   Now word before long was brought to the bishop
Of that bright buried body and its blazing, strange wonders.
(The good man himself had gone off on a journey.
In Essex they found him, inspecting an abbey.)   *county near London*
When they told him the tale of the uncovered tomb,
How men clattered and chaffered concerning the corpse,   110
The bishop sent beadles to quiet the bother,
And followed himself with his household and horses.
As his party approached Saint Paul's church and its precincts,
Men hastened to him to rehearse this great marvel,
But he called out for peace and passed into his palace.
Ignoring their news, he then fastened the door.
The dark night drew on till the day-bell was rung,
But the saint arose sooner, long before dawn.
Well-nigh all that night he had made his entreaties,
Beseeching his Sovereign of His sweetest grace   120
To vouchsafe a vision revealing the truth.
"Though I am unworthy"—and he wept as he said this—
"Through the might of His mercy may my dearest Lord,
Confirming Christ's covenant, cause me to know
The truth of this mystery men marvel over."
As he prayed and implored there, God granted him grace:
The Holy Ghost answered as morning grew light.
Then men opened the minster, Matins were said,   *morning prayers*
And Erkenwald readied himself for the rites.

In pontifical robes the prelate prepared.   130
Next, the man and his ministers said the great Mass
That sings of the Spirit that works in the world,   *the Mass of the Holy Spirit*
While the choir chanted coolly in intricate tones.
Many a great one gathered to hear them
(For the bravest of barons frequented Saint Paul's),
Till the last words were said and the service was ceased.
Then away from the altar the celebrants wound.
   When the prelate went past them, the barons all bowed,
As, still richly arrayed, he strode straight to the tomb.
Some unlocked the cloister with clusters of keys,   140
And pinched was the press of men passing inside.
The bishop came to the burial with a body of barons
And the mayor and his men, with mace-bearers before them.
The dean of the church described the discovery,
Pointing to show the appropriate place.
"Lo, lords," he said, "the body beside me
Has lain here long years now—their number's unknown—
Yet his color and clothes are clearly unharmed,
Like his corpse and the casket enclosing it all.
No lord in the land has lived here so long   150
That his mind can remember when such a man reigned
Or name us his name or his doings of note,
And yet many a poor man interred in this place
Is recalled in our records both now and forever.
We have leafed through our library seven full days:
Yet no chronicle casts the least light on this lord.
He's not lain here so long though, to judge by his looks,
As to pass out of memory, melt from our minds."
"So it is," said the saintly one, blessed by the church,
"Yet this marvel to men mounts to nothing at all   160
Beside the power of the prince who patrols Paradise
When He's pleased to display the least part of His might.
Although men stand amazed and unsure in their minds,
And their reasons are rent and truth rests out of reach,
The force of God's finger frees much greater things
That no hands under heaven might ever heave loose.
Where the creatures' best counsel cannot prevail
The Savior Himself must present us the cure.

We've done all we can here; divine we no more.
Earthly truth-seeking will never suffice.   170
Let us call on God, rather, to give us His grace,
For He's kindly of counsel and comforts the meek,
Confirming their confidence, crowning their faith.
Now I'll tell you so truly the tale of this man
You'll believe with me, lords, that our God is right great
And wills to reward all who walk in His love."
The saint turned to the tomb then and talked to the corpse,
Lifting its eyelids, he appealed to it thus:
"Sir, long as you've lain here, lie still no longer,
For Jesus has judged that His joy shall be shown.   180
Keep His command, for I call in His name.
He was killed on the Cross at the cost of His blood,
As you may have seen, sir, and we still believe.
Now answer me honestly, withholding no truths.
Your name is not known here. Announce it yourself—
What you were in the world, too, and why you lie thus.
How long have you lain here? What belief did you hold?
Were you granted God's grace, or go you in pain?"
Thus the saint had his say, and sighed as he said it.
Then the corpse in the casket made a creaking, small noise,   190
Through the ghost-life God gave it by His guiding will,
And with unhappy accent it uttered these words:
"My lord," said the corpse, "I receive your charge gladly.
I'd keep your command if it cost me my eyes.
The name that you named here and summoned me by
Rules heaven and hell and the world poised between.
First, I'll tell you in truth what I was when alive—
The most unfortunate fellow found on the earth:
No sovereign nor count nor yet noble knight,
But a liege of the law that belonged to us then.   200
I managed men's matters, a magistrate here;
Hearing pleas and disputes, I prescribed to the city
For my patron, a prince of the pagan regime.
I and my fellows all followed his faith.
But to time my interment is too much for me;
I've lain here too long now for plain men to measure.

After Brutus first founded his fledgling new city,   *London's legendary founder*
Five centuries, less eighteen, were immured in the past   *482 years*
Before the coming of Christ by your Christian account.
And then five hundred thirty and three times eight more   *554 years*
I spent in this sepulture, shut from salvation.
The rich reigning king who ruled over me—
Was the Breton Belinus, with Brennius his brother.
Ample affronts each of those gave his sibling,
Those battling brothers, while their broils persisted.
And I was a judge firmly joined to the law."
　　While the corpse was discoursing, the concourse of people
Said nothing—no dinning nor banter nor noise.
All stood like stones as they somberly listened,
Mute with amazement, though many were weeping.   220
The bishop broke silence by bidding the body:
"If you were no king, who consigned you this crown?
And why do you wield a great scepter, we wonder,
When no liege men loyally pledged you their lives?"
"Dear bishop," said the body, "be easy on this.
Unsought were these signs that surround my corpse now.
I levied the laws under loftier lords,
Yet I was the arch-judge in charge of this place
And ruled this rich town in the most righteous wise,
Fulfilling my faith over forty long years.   230
False felons and ruffians afoul of the law,
I struck them down sternly to soften their wills.
But neither for weal nor for wealth nor for wrath,
Not for mastery nor money nor any man's might,
Did I relinquish the right as I ruled it to be
Or torture the truth as I tendered my verdicts
Or corrupt my best conscience for covetous ends.
My judgments were genuine, honest and just.
I ruled the rich rightly, deferring to none.
No menace nor mischief, compassion nor grief,   240
Could sway me to swerve from the high road of right,
The facts that good faith had confirmed in my heart.
One who murdered my father got justice from me;
Nor would I favor my father to free him from hanging.

Because I was righteous regarding the law,
Dole for my death caused a din in New Troy.
All lamented their loss, both lesser and great ones,
And to burnish my body they brought out their gold.
They clothed me most cleanly in courtliest clothes;
Mantled me as the most matchless man on the bench;   250
Girded me as governor and guide of the city;
Furred me as the finest of faith of my kind.
To honor my honesty and high enterprise,
They crowned me as king of my kindred at law
That New Troy had known then or ever would know.
Then to attest to my truthfulness they allowed me this scepter."
    The bishop asked after that, uneasy at heart,
How, though men buried the body in the brightest of robes,
It chanced that its clothes were still clean, for "in rags,"
Said the saint, "all these clothes should be clotted.   260
Though well-meaning men may have embalmed your good body
So no rot or rank worms have corrupted it yet,
Still, your color and clothes . . . I cannot see how
They have lain here so long and lasted so well."
"No," said the body, "I was never embalmed.
No common conveyance has kept me from harm.
The Regent of Reason, who revels in right
And loves all good laws that belong to the truth,
Protects His retainers who tread the just path
Over others who use lesser virtues in life.   270
While men may have made my magnificent clothes,
It was Christ, sir, who kept me uncorrupt as I am."
    "Yet speak," said the saint, "of the state of your soul.
Where does it wander, if your life was so just?
He who rewards all who hew to the right
Must have given you, surely, a glimpse of His grace,
For He says in his psalms of His servants on earth:
'All pure and impartial men, muster to Me.'[3]
So speak of your soul in the state where it dwells
And the rich restitution it received from Our Lord."   280

3. Perhaps a paraphrase of Psalm 15:1–2.

The corpse coughed in its casket, wagging its head.
It gave a great groan before God and then said:
"Mighty Maker of men, thy mercies are great,
But how could you honor a heathen like me—
An unready wretch not enrolled in your law,
Unaware of your word or the weight of your power?
I was feeble and faithless, uninformed of the rules
By which you were worshipped. Oh woe worth the day!
I was none of that number your anguish has saved,
Bought with your blood as you bent from the Cross.   290
When you harried the hell-halls, reclaiming your folk—
Your lieges from Limbo—you left me to languish,
And there sits my soul yet. It still sees no farther,
Drowned in dark death that derives from our parent,
Adam, our elder, who ate of the apple.
Though blameless, we bide here, made ill by his error.
You Christians were singed by his sin and corruption,
But a marvelous medicine mended your lot—
Bountiful baptism buoyed you from sin.
No solace like that for myself and my soul.   300
What did we win with our wisdom and righteousness,
When we're dolefully damned in the deepest of pits,
And shut from God's supper, that solemn, great feast
Where those hungry for justice receive their reward?
My soul must sit sadly, suffering in sickness,
Where dark never yields to the dimmest of dawns.
She is held fast in hell, where she hungers for meals
With nothing to nourish her, no help for her woes."

　　The dead man so dolefully described his great sorrows
That all wept for woe upon hearing his words,   310
And the bishop stood brooding, eyes bent to the floor.
He scarcely could speak for his throat was constricted,
So he stood still a space and surveyed the rich tomb
And the body below, as he blinked back his tears.
"May God bid," said the bishop, "that you bide with us here,
For the time that it takes to fetch water to serve us,
To cast on your corpse while recounting these words:
'I christen thee in the company of Christ and the Father

And the Holy Ghost'—and not one instant more—
And then drop into death, for true death is your due."   320
As these words welled within him, the water of weeping—
His warm tears—trilled down on the man and his tomb.
When one fell on his face, the corpse sighed again
And whispered in wonder: "Salute now the Savior!
Praise be to great God and to His gracious mother!
And blessed be the most blissful hour that she bore Him!
And bless you too, bishop, for lifting my burden,
Relieving the loss that I lived with before.
For your worshipful words and the water you spilled,
Your eyes' precious bounty, have baptized my soul!   330
The first drop you dropped here dispelled my long sorrow.
At last in God's love I'm enlightened and fed.
With your words and the water to wash away sins
A lightning flash lit all the lower abyss
And my weary soul swiftly sprang up with delight
To sit in God's supper-room, solemn and true.
A marshal there met her with marvelous honors.
He reverently offered her room evermore.
I honor high God here, and you as well, bishop.
You have brought me to bliss. Let me blazon your worth!"   340
    The dead man's sound ceased and he said nothing more,
But his wholesome looks wavered and withered away.
His blessed, bright body grew blacker than mold,
As rank as old rottenness rising in powder.
For as soon as his soul had been summoned to bliss,
His flesh dried to foulness enfolding his bones.
Just so, God's lasting life that delights souls forever
Soon voids flesh's vainglory that so little avails us.
The men lifted their love of Our Lord to the heavens.
Mourning and mirth mingled then in their hearts.   350
They passed out in procession, joined by the people,
As the town filled with thanks and the tolling of bells.

THE COCK AND THE FOX

ROBERT HENRYSON

This is one of thirteen beast fables by Robert Henryson (c. 1425–c. 1500), perhaps the most accomplished Scottish poet of the fifteenth century. The author was reportedly the schoolmaster of Dunfermline, the ancient Scottish capital near Edinburgh, where he also served as a notary and probably practiced law. He is best known for his Testament of Cresseid, *an able continuation of Chaucer's* Troilus and Cressida, *but he left a considerable body of other works, including the* Fabillis *and a retelling of the Orpheus and Eurydice myth.*

The beast-fable tradition goes back to Aesop, a Greek slave of the seventh century BC, but Henryson's immediate source was Chaucer's "Nun's Priest's Tale," which he shortened and simplified, leaving out, for instance, Chaucer's philosophical comments on free will and determinism in favor of a broader sort of humor as the "widowed" hens comment on Chanticleer's sexual performance.

As with Chaucer, a great deal of Henryson's appeal rests in his style, a deft combination of lightness and psychological insight. It's always fun to be on hand as beasts send up human foibles, especially if they do it in brisk and elegant verse. The form of the poem is Chaucerian as well—rhyme royal, the seven-line stanza Chaucer used to such great effect in Troilus and Cressida.

Although the lower beasts are all irrational—
Incapable of human calculation—
Each one of them as far as it is natural
Must act within its native inclination:
Boar, wolf, and lion breathe determination;
The fox is false and crafty, as is right;
And dogs are bred to guard and bark at night.

So different are they in their properties—
Unknown to us and almost infinite—
Their blood gives rise to such diversities,   10
To write them down would far exceed my wit.
For now, then, I draw in the field a bit

And tell an old tale that I chanced to hear
About a fox and noble Chanticleer.

A simple village widow of those days
Spun yarn to feed herself and her small stock.
She had right little, sirs, my story says,
Except some hens, who formed her modest flock,
And then to serve her hens a handsome cock.
He served the widow too another way—   20
Crowed through the night and to proclaim each day.

Not very far from this poor widow's place
There stood a thorny thicket dark and dense,
Where lived a cunning fox, both sly and base—
His chief resort and daily residence.
This fox had caused the widow great expense
By pilfering her chickens day and night.
Nor could she catch him, try to as she might.

The fox, named Lawrence, heard the first lark's song
And slunk into the widow's yard, the pest.   30
There Chanticleer patrolled the still, gray dawn,
Where, tired of night, he'd flown down from his rest.
Lawrence saw, and in his mind he cast
For stratagems to charm his strutting foe,
Disarm the cock, and win his dinner so.

So, hiding his true countenance and cheer,
He fell upon his knees, and thus he said:
"Good morning, master, gentle Chanticleer!"
At that, the cock jumped backward like a maid.
"Sir," said the fox, "I pray, don't be afraid.   40
Don't shrink away, I beg you, sir, or flee.
I've come to do you service, as you'll see.

"If not, indeed, I would be much to blame,
I honored, sir, your great progenitors.
Your father often fed me fruit and game,
Sent food to me across the fields and moors,

And at his end I served as his best nurse.
I held his head, gave comfort, kept him warm,
Until at last he perished in my arms."

"You knew him then?" the cock said in surprise.   50
"I did, my son—I held his drooping head
Beneath a birch, and later closed his eyes,
And sang the solemn dirge when he was dead.
What feud could be between us?" the fox said.
"Whom should you trust but me, your honest friend,
Who gave your father honor to his end?

"When I behold your feathers, noble sir—
Your beak, your breast, your hackles, and your comb—
Then, by my soul and all that I hold dear,
My heart is warmed as if I had come home.   60
To serve you, lord, I'd crawl across the loam
Through frost and snow, beneath the rain and sleet,
And lay my grizzled locks beneath your feet!"

But then the fox, whose subtlety was great,
Mixed with his praise this crafty reservation:
"You seem, my lord, diminished in your state
From your great father's high and matchless station.
For crowing here or, sir, throughout the nation,
He bore the crown, for he would rise and crow
Upon his toes. I saw him, and I know."   70

With that the cock stood up upon his toes,
Thrust forth his beak, and sang with all his might.
"Well sung, my lord," said Lawrence; "Now heaven knows
You are your father's son. You're his of right.
Yet not quite perfect—though the fault is slight:
For when your father sang, without a doubt,
He'd close his eyes and twirl himself about."

The cock, puffed up with hollow vanity,
That puts too many hearts in danger's way,
Trusting to win worship, as you see,   80
Shut both his eyes and made a great display

Of hems and hums before he'd sing away.
But suddenly, before he crowed a note,
The fox leapt up and snatched him by the throat!

Then to the wood full lightly Lawrence fled.
No one could stop him now along his route.
Pertok, Sprutok, and Coppok shrieked and pled;   *the hens' names*
The widow heard and crying loud ran out.
She saw how matters stood and gave a shout:
"Murder!" she called so everyone could hear.   90
"The fox has carried off my Chanticleer!"

As if insane, with many a yelp and cry,
She pulled her hair and beat upon her breast.
And then all pale, half in an ecstasy,
She fell down grieving, sweating and oppressed.
With that, the widow's hens rose off their nests
And, while the woman lay there in her fit,
Began to sound the case with all their wit.

"Alas," said Pertok, dreadful in her mourning—
The brimming tears ran down her cheeks and fell—   100
"He was prosperity, our daily darling,
Our nightingale and love, our morning bell,
Our watchful ward, for he would wake and tell
When mild Aurora with her kerchief gray   *dawn*
Put up her head between the night and day.

"Who shall our lover be? Who shall us lead?
When we are sad, my sisters, who shall sing?
With his sweet bill, I've seen him break our bread.
In all the world was there a finer thing?
In making love he'd mount our backs and cling   110
With all his skill, as nature showed him how.
Our lord is gone. What hope can we have now?"

Then Sprutok said, "Now, sister, cease your sorrow.
You're wrong to mourn so, for as heaven knows,
Saint John's wise words should steel us for the morrow:

His proverb says, 'All goodness comes and goes.'
So I for one will don my finest clothes
And make me fresh—for it's still jolly May—
And sing, 'I'm widowed now, but yet I'm gay!'

"He was a tyrant, and he held us low,   120
And rough and jealous too, if I don't lie.
At loving sport, my Pertok, as you know,
He was a weak performer, cold and dry.
Now that he's gone, my dear, you mustn't cry.
Be blithe in sorrow now his life has fled.
Let quick be quick, and let the dead be dead."

Pertok replied (her grief was false before,
For lust, not love, had been her whole delight),
"My dear, you know of such as him a score
Would be too few to slake our appetite.   130
I pledge here by my hand that you are right;
Within a week we'll have much finer cheer—
Some better cock to thump us on the rear."

Then Coppok spoke, disdainful as a curate:
"I hold this whole affair is heaven's plan.
He was so lewd! I hardly could endure it.
He kept," she said, "a wench on every hand.
But good God tries the weight of every man,
And He strikes hard, before His wrath is spent,
Adulterers who choose not to repent.   140

"Our lord was proud, rejoicing in his sin,
Indifferent to God's anger or His grace.
He meant to please himself yet save his skin.
But now at last his vices show their face.
This shameful end has put him in his place.
Lo, here we see God smites before He knocks,
For God it was who gave him to the fox."

When this was said, the widow from her swoon
Leaped to her feet and called her hounds, each one:

"How, Birky, Berry, Bausie, Bell, and Bruin!   150
Up, Ripshaw, Runwell, Curtis, Stint-for-none!
Together then, with all your hearts, now run!
Save my noble cock before he's slain,
Or else run on and don't come back again!"

With that, hell-bent, hounds hallooed through the heather;
Like fire from flint they flew across the field.
Swift as swallows sail through stormy weather,
They madly made for Lawrence, unconcealed.
The fox was tired. As they came on, he reeled.
He thought less of his heavy captive then: 160
"God grant," he said, "we make it to my den!"

The cock spoke up, by some good sprite inspired,
"Now listen, fox, and have the last laugh yet.
Although you're hot and hungry, sir, and tired,
Grown faint of force and drowning in your sweat,
Turn back to them all easy with, 'Well met!
This cock and I are friends. He won't deny it.'
We'll fool them, if you're fox enough to try it!"

The fox, although a false and knowing liar,
With trick on trick, some underhand, some bold,   170
Was fooled himself, and by his own desire,
For falseness fails as men have found of old.
He loosed his grip to speak as he'd been told,
And, lo, the cock flew up onto a bough.
Who thinks the hapless fox is laughing now?

Beguiled this way, the fox beneath the tree
Dropped to his knees and said, "Good Chanticleer,
Come down again and I, sir, as you'll see,
Shall be your servant, bound-man for a year."
"No, killer, thief, and villain, never fear: 180
My bloody hackles and my bruised neck too
Have banished my love between us two.

"I closed my eyes! My vanity was stirred.
And by that fault I almost lost my head!"

"Yet I was worse," the fox said, "on my word,
For I did as you told me out of dread."
"Go feed on someone else," the rooster said.
Then, seeing that the fox had no reply,
He winged his way back home across the sky.

The Moral

Now, worthy folk, although this is a fable   190
With beasts that talk, as real ones never do,
Think just a bit and you will find you're able,
Even so, to glean a truth or two.
For Chanticleer's an image, I hope true,
Of men who grow toplofty and vainglorious
Because their blood is blue, or just notorious.

Fie, puffed-up pride, for you are full of death.
Who favors you perforce must have a fall.
Your strength is naught; you waver with each breath,
As devils show, who through the pride of all   200
Were hounded down from heaven's gracious hall
To hideous hell, that dark and burning hole.
Such rebels show how pride exacts its toll.

The evil, scheming fox may represent
These flatterers who work with hidden spite.
With double minds, fair words unkindly meant,
They fool their prey, for such is their delight.
All worthy folk should hold them in despite,
For what could be a worse, more fatal course
Than listening to lies from such a source?   210

The wicked savor of false adulation—
Sweet as sugar in similitude—
Turns sour at last. It makes a fatal ration
To all who taste when rightly understood.
And therefore, people, briefly to conclude:
This pair of sins—to flatter and be vain—
    Are venomous. They bring us endless pain.

Appendixes

APPENDIX A

BIBLIOGRAPHY

Indexes of Middle English Verse

Boffey, Julia, and A. S. G. Edwards. *A New Index of Middle English Verse.* London: British Library, 2005. [Supercedes Brown and Robbins' *Index* and Robbins and Cutler's *Supplement.*]

Brown, Carleton, and Rossell Hope Robbins. *Index of Middle English Verse.* New York: Index Society, 1943.

Ringler, William A. *Bibliography and Index of English Verse in Manuscript, 1501–1558.* London and New York: Mansell, 1992. [Ringler MS Index]

———. *Bibliography and Index of English Verse Printed 1476–1558.* London and New York: Mansell, 1988. [Ringler Printed Index]

Robbins, Rossell Hope, and John L. Cutler. *Supplement to the Index of Middle English Verse.* Lexington: U of Kentucky P, 1965.

Sources for the Texts

Athelston. In Sands, below.

Burrow, J. A., and Thorlac Turville-Petre, eds. *A Book of Middle English.* 2nd ed. Oxford and Cambridge, MA: Blackwell, 1996.

Davies, R. T., ed. *Medieval English Lyrics: A Critical Anthology.* Evanston: Northwestern UP, 1964.

Douglas, Gavin. *The Aeneid of Virgil, Translated into Scottish Verse.* Reprint of 1839 ed. New York: AMS Press, 1971.

Duncan, Thomas G., ed. *Medieval English Lyrics, 1200–1400.* London: Penguin, 1995.

Dunn, Charles W., and Edward T. Byrnes, eds. *Middle English Literature.* Revised ed. New York and London: Garland, 1990.

Gower, John. *Selections from John Gower.* Edited by J. A. W. Bennett. Oxford: Clarendon P, 1968.

Henryson, Robert. *The Poems of Robert Henryson.* Edited by Robert L. Kindrick. Kalamazoo: Medieval Institute, 1997.

Ker, N. R., ed. *Facsimile of British Museum MS. Harley 2253.* Early English Text Society. London: Oxford UP, 1965.

The Land of Cockayne. In Dunn and Byrnes, above.

Langland, William. *The Vision of Piers Plowman.* Edited by A. V. C. Schmidt. London and New York: Dent and E. P. Dutton, 1978.

Luria, Maxwell S., and Richard L. Hoffman, eds. *Middle English Lyrics.* Norton Critical Edition. New York and London: Norton, 1974.

Robbins, Rossell Hope, ed. *Secular Lyrics of the XIVth and XVth Centuries.* 2nd ed. Oxford: Clarendon P, 1968.

Saint Erkenwald. In Burrow and Turville-Petre, above.

Sands, Donald B., ed. *Middle English Verse Romances.* New York: Holt, Rinehart and Winston, 1966.

Sir Orfeo. In Burrow and Turville-Petre, above.

Sisam, Kenneth and Celia, eds. *The Oxford Book of Medieval English Verse.* Oxford: Clarendon P, 1970.

The Squire of Low Degree. In Sands, above.

Stevick, Robert D., ed. *One Hundred Middle English Lyrics.* Rev. ed. Urbana and Chicago: U Illinois P, 1994.

Criticism

Barron, W. R. *English Medieval Romance.* London: Longman, 1987.

Bennett, J. A. W. *Middle English Literature: The Oxford History of English Literature,* vol. 1, part 2. Edited and completed by Douglas Gray. Oxford: Oxford UP, 1986.

Boitani, Piero. "Introduction: An Idea of Fourteenth-Century Literature." In Boitani and Torti, below.

Boitani, Piero, and Anna Torti, eds. *Literature in Fourteenth-Century England: The J. A. W. Bennett Memorial Lectures, Perugia, 1981–1982.* Tübingen and Cambridge: Gunter Narr and D. S. Brewer, 1983.

Bolton, W. F., ed. *The Middle Ages.* New York: Peter Bedrick, 1987.

Burrow, J. A. *Essays on Medieval Literature.* Oxford: Clarendon P, 1984.

———. *Medieval Writers and Their Work: Middle English Literature and Its Background, 1100–1500.* Oxford: Oxford UP, 1982.

Davenport, W. A. *Medieval Narrative: An Introduction.* Oxford: Oxford UP, 2004.

Duncan, Thomas G., ed. *A Companion to Middle English.* Cambridge: D. S. Brewer, 2005.

Fisher, John H. *John Gower: Moral Philosopher and Friend of Chaucer.* New York: New York UP, 1964.

Godden, Malcolm. *The Making of Piers Plowman.* London: Longman, 1990.

Gray, Douglas. "Later Poetry: The Courtly Tradition." In Bolton, above.

———. *Robert Henryson.* Medieval and Renaissance Authors. Leiden: Brill, 1979.

———. "Songs and Lyrics." In Boitani and Torti, above.

———. *Themes and Images in the Medieval Religious Lyric.* London: Routledge & Kegan Paul, 1972.

Greentree, Rosemary. *The Middle English Lyric and Short Poem.* Cambridge: D. S. Brewer, 2001.

Krueger, Roberta L. *Cambridge Companion to Medieval Romance.* Cambridge: Cambridge UP, 2000.

Lawlor, John. *Piers Plowman: An Essay in Criticism.* London: E. Arnold, 1962.

Mehl, Dieter. *English Literature in the Age of Chaucer.* London: Longman, 2001.

Mills, Maldwyn, Jennifer Fellows, and Carol M. Meale, eds. *Romance in Medieval England.* Cambridge: D. S. Brewer, 1991.

Salter, Elizabeth. *Piers Plowman: An Introduction.* Oxford: Blackwell, 1962.

Shepherd, G. T. "Early Middle English Literature." In Bolton, above.

Stevens, John. *Words and Music in the Middle Ages: Song, Narrative, Dance and Drama, 1050–1350.* Rev. ed. Cambridge: Cambridge UP, 1986.

Turville-Petre, Thorlac. *The Alliterative Revival.* Cambridge: D. S. Brewer, 1987.

Wallace, David, ed. *The Cambridge History of Medieval English Literature.* Cambridge: Cambridge UP, 1999.

Williams, J. D. "Alliterative Poetry in the Fourteenth and Fifteenth Centuries." In Bolton, above.

Wilson, R. M. *The Lost Literature of Medieval England.* New York: Cooper Square, 1969.

Woolf, Rosemary. *The English Religious Lyric in the Middle Ages.* Oxford: Clarendon P, 1968.

———. "Later Poetry: The Popular Tradition." In Bolton, above.

Yeager, R. F. *John Gower's Poetic: The Search for a New Arion.* Cambridge: D. S. Breuer, 1990.

APPENDIX B

FIRST LINES, SOURCES, AND INDEX NUMBERS

The poems are listed by item number, not page number, and the first lines are standardized according to A New Index of Middle English Verse. *First lines given here correspond closely to those appearing in the indexes of Brown and Robbins, Robbins and Cutler, and also Ringler. The lines are generally abbreviated, but there should be enough information in every case to find the item in one of the indexes.*

Poems with burdens or refrains are alphabetized by the first word of the running text, not the refrain. Whole numbers show that the work appears in both A New Index *and Brown and Robbins. Numbers carried out to one decimal indicate an item first appeared in Robbins and Cutler's Supplement. Two decimal places mean the work's first mention came in Boffey and Edwards.*

I have not tried to list every modern collection in which each poem appears, just to provide references for anyone wanting to see the original text in one of these anthologies:

NORTON   Luria, Maxwell S., and Richard L. Hoffman, eds. *Middle English Lyrics.* Norton Critical Edition. New York and London: Norton, 1974.

PENGUIN   Duncan, Thomas G., ed. *Medieval English Lyrics, 1200–1400.* London: Penguin, 1995.

ROBBINS   Robbins, Rossell Hope, ed. *Secular Lyrics of the XIVth and XVth Centuries.* 2nd ed. Oxford: Clarendon P, 1968.

SISAM   Sisam, Kenneth and Celia, eds. *The Oxford Book of Medieval English Verse.* Oxford: Clarendon P, 1970.

STEVICK   Stevick, Robert D., ed. *One Hundred Middle English Lyrics.* Rev. ed. Urbana and Chicago: U Illinois P, 1994.

		Index Number	Source
1	Svmer is icumen in	3223	Norton 3, Penguin 110
2	Al nist by þ[e] rose rose	194	Norton 17, Robbins 17
3	Bytuene mersh ant aueril	515	Norton 27, Penguin 18
4	Of eureykune tre	2622	Penguin 9, Robbins 16
5	Goo Iytell ryngg	932	Robbins 95
6	Bryd one brere brid	521	Norton 22, Robbins 147
7	O lord of loue here	2491	Robbins 128
8	Go, litull bill, and command	Ringler Printed 474	Norton 55, Robbins 194
9	Now wold I fayn sum	2381	Norton 53, Robbins 171
10	The smyling mouth	3465	Norton 24, Robbins 184
11	My gostly fader I me	2243	Norton 25, Robbins 185
12	I pray you, M,	Ringler MS 677	Robbins 193
13	Gracius and gay	1010	Norton 46, Robbins 143
14	I have a gentil cok	1299	Norton 77, Robbins 46
15	Haue gooday nou mergerete	1121	Norton 23, Robbins 149
16	My deþ y loue	2236	Norton 34, Penguin 24
17	I pray you cum kysse me	Ringler MS 97	Norton 79, Sisam 245
18	In a fryht as y con	1449	Norton 30, Penguin 22
19	We bern abowtyn	3864	Norton 81, Robbins 7
20	In all this warld	1468	Norton 82, Robbins 8
21	O mestress, why	Ringler MS 1206	Norton 45, Robbins 137
22	Hogyn cam to bowers	Ringler MS 601	Norton 80, Robbins 36

		Index Number	Source
23	Lenten ys come	1861	Norton 4, Robbins 48
24	Foweles in the frith	864	Norton 6, Penguin 16
25	I have a newe gardyn	1302	Norton 78, Robbins 21
26	The man that I loued	3418	Norton 56, Robbins 22
27	Y louede a child	1330	Norton 57, Robbins 23
28	I am olde whan age	Ringler MS 630	Norton 71, Robbins 176
29	Vuto you most froward	Ringler MS 1760	Norton 72, Robbins 208
30	O lord, so swett	2494	Norton 85, Robbins 26
31	As I went on Yol day	377	Norton 86, Robbins 27
32	When þe nyhtegale singes	4037	Norton 35, Penguin 17
33	My cares comen euer anew	2231	Norton 47, Robbins 150
34	O kendly creature	2475	Robbins 153
35	Go hert hurt with	925	Norton 49, Robbins 155
36	My lefe ys faren	2254	Robbins 160
37	This ys no lyf alas	3613	Norton 243, Robbins 165
38	Wer þer ouþer in þis	3898	Norton 37, Robbins 9
39	When nettuls in wynter	3999	Norton 63, Robbins 114
40	In euery place ye may	1485	Norton 62, Robbins 38
41	Ying men I warne you	4279	Norton 68, Robbins 43
42	To onpreise wemen	3782	Norton 40, Robbins 34
43	I am sory for her sake	1280	Norton 41, Robbins 37
44	Bring us in no browne	549	Norton 159, Robbins 13
45	D . . . dronken	694.11	Norton 163, Robbins 117
46	Omnes gentes plaudite	2675	Norton 157, Robbins 5

		INDEX NUMBER	SOURCE
47	Is tell you my mind	Ringler MS 826	Norton 158, Robbins 6
48	Kynge I syt	1822	Penguin 59, Sisam 86
49	Nowe ys Yngland	2335	Sisam 201
50	Trvsty. seldom to their	Ringler MS 1776	Robbins 110
51	Blowyng was mad for gret	543	Sisam 214
52	I am a fol i can no god	1269	Sisam 89
53	Allas what schul we freris do	161	Penguin 131, Sisam 172
54	Deceyt deceyuyth	674	Robbins 107
55	Allas dicyte þat in trust	145	Robbins 108
56	Mirie it is while summer ilast	2163	Norton 5, Penguin 36
57	Bi a forrest as y gan fare	559	Norton 134, Robbins 119
58	I herd a carpyng of a clerk	1317	Sisam 194
59	It fell ageyns the next night	1622	Norton 135, Robbins 48
60	Let no man cum	Ringler MS 884	Norton 144, Robbins 2
61	The bores hed in hondes	Ringler MS 1502	Norton 153, Robbins 55
62	Owre kynge went forth	2716	Sisam 151, Stevick 51
63	A dere God what may	5	Sisam 130
64	Lyarde es ane olde horse	2026	Sisam 167
65	Sum men sayon þat	3174	Norton 139, Robbins 33
66	At the northe ende	438	Norton 89, Robbins 30
67	I have twelve oxen	Ringler MS 649	Norton 133, Robbins 47
68	Þe formest of þese bestes	3353	Sisam 289

		Index Number	Source
69	Swarte smekyd semthes	3227	Norton 140, Robbins 118
70	I have a yong suster	1303	Norton 137, Robbins 45
71	Maiden in the mor lay	2037.5	Norton 138, Robbins 18
72	I have been a foster	Ringler MS 643	Sisam 246
73	XXXti days hath novembre	3571	Norton 106, Robbins 68
74	By thys fyre	579	Norton 108, Robbins 67
75	Giff sanct Paullis day	1423	Norton 110, Robbins 71
76	XXXII teth that beþh	3572	Norton 111, Robbins 75
77	Sluggy & slowe	3157	Norton 112, Robbins 76
78	Juce of lekes	1810	Norton 114, Robbins 80
79	Spend and God schal sende	3209	Norton 118, Robbins 60
80	I had my syluer	1297	Norton 123
81	Pees maketh plente	2742	Norton 124, Robbins 84
82	Kepe well x & flee	1817	Norton 131, Robbins 83
83	Gode sire pray ich þe	1008	Norton 143, Robbins 15
84	Here lyeth under this	1207	Norton 245, Robbins 124
85	Al gold Jonet	179	Penguin 11
86	Merie singen þe munaches	2164	Sisam 264
87	Thei thou the wulf	3513 [May be prose]	Sisam 278
88	A man may a while	Ringler MS 25	Sisam 281
89	King conseilles	1820	Sisam 283
90	Wake wel annot	3859.5	Sisam 285
91	Hope is hard	1251	Sisam 292

		INDEX NUMBER	SOURCE
92	The ax was sharpe	3306	Sisam 299
93	Whan adam delf	3922	Sisam 300
94	Whan bloweþ þe brom	3927.6	Sisam 301
95	Be hit beter be hit werse	465.5	Sisam 306
96	The smaller pesun	3464.5	Sisam 307
97	Two wimin in one house	Ringler MS 1779	Sisam 309
98	Þre is none so wyse man	3538	Sisam 310
99	Walterius Pollard	Not indexed	Sisam 316
100	Thys boke is one	3580	Robbins 90, Sisam 317
101	Her I was and her I drank	1201	Norton 162, Robbins 12
102	Þer ys no merth	3533.5	Sisam 321
103	Brissit brawnis and	Not indexed	Sisam 330
104	Chyldern profyt[1]	597.5	Sisam 332
105	Ne saltou neuer[2]	2288	Penguin 12
106	Hou shold y with	1265	Penguin 26
107	Murie a tyme	2162	Robbins 141
108	Say me viit in þe brom	3078	Norton 61, Penguin 111
109	Say, wight y the brom[3]	Not indexed	Penguin 111
110	Know er thow knytte	1829	Norton 65, Robbins 40
111	Adam lay Ibowndyn	117	Norton 164, Penguin 108

1. There are four separate riddles in this brief collection, among them "Alison" and "Isabel."

2. This text contains three separate short poems—or perhaps passages from poems. "Door, open softly" is the third.

3. After giving the preceding "wight in the broom" poem in the text, the Penguin editor quotes this variant in his explanatory note (p. 239).

		Index Number	Source
112	I haue laborede	1308	Norton 231
113	Loue me brouthe	2012	Norton 219, Penguin 70
114	I am iesu þat cum	1274	Norton 220, Penguin 72
115	Senful man be þing	3109	Norton 215
116	Seynt Steuene was a clerk	3058	Penguin 126, Sisam 31
117	O mankynde	2507	Stevick 92
118	Ihesu crist my lemmon	1684	Sisam 95
119	Suete ihesu king of blysse	3236	Norton 92, Penguin 67
120	Louerd þu clepedest me	1978	Norton 93, Penguin 49
121	This endrys nyght	3596	Sisam 212
122	Wyth was hys nakede	4088	Penguin 85, Sisam 4
123	Þu sikest sore	3691	Penguin 93, Sisam 85
124	Lullay Lullay litel child	2023	Norton 202, Penguin 82
125	I syng of a myden þat	1367	Norton 181, Penguin 79
126	Nou goth þe sonne	2320	Norton 190, Penguin 84
127	Ther is no rose	3536	Sisam 169
128	Of on þat is so fayr	2645	Penguin 75
129	Vpon a lady my loue	3836	Norton 188
130	Als i lay vpon a nith	353	Norton 198
131	A schelde of red	91	Sisam 270
132	A Man þat xuld	72	Sisam 186
133	Anoder yere hyt may betyde	320	Stevick 95
134	Goo litle book of	929	Robbins 104
135	Steddefast crosse inmong	3212	Norton 209, Penguin 103
136	Worldes blis ne last	4223	Norton 1, Penguin 38

Index Number		Source
137	Yche day me cumeþ	695	Penguin 41
138	In þe vale of abraham	1568	Stevick 55
139	Here I ame and fourthe	1199	Norton 128, Robbins 64
140	All ye that passe	Ringler MS 125	Norton 244, Robbins 126
141	Vpon my Ryght syde	3844	Sisam 226
142	A cros was maad	Not indexed	Robbins 101
143	God [sic] & al þis	1002	Norton 15, Penguin 96
144	When erþ haþ earþ	3939	Norton 242, Penguin 55
145	I Wende to dede	1387	Norton 241, Stevick 87
146	Wen þe turuf is þi tuur	4044	Norton 232, Penguin 45
147	Kyndeli is now mi coming	1818	Norton 237
148	If man him biþocte	1422	Norton 233, Penguin 43
149	Þe blessinge of heuene	3310	Stevick 18
150	I hadde richesse	1298	Stevick 88
151	Was there never caren	Not indexed	Penguin 57
152	Wynter wakeneþ all my care	4177	Norton 13, Penguin 52
153	This winde be reson	Ringler MS 1674	Norton 166
154	Euen it es a rich ture	1179	Norton 180
155	A God and yet a man	37	Norton 197
156	Wreche man why art	4239	Norton 239, Penguin 56
157	Lully, lulley, lully	Ringler MS 530	Norton 230, Sisam 247

Appendix C

Alphabetical List of First Lines

This list includes only those poems in the first three sections—"Worldly Lyrics," "Snatches," and "Religious Lyrics." In poems with burdens or refrains the first lines of these are listed as well, in italics.